Frank Lloyd Wright's
FALLINGWATER
The House and Its History

DONALD HOFFMANN

WITH AN INTRODUCTION BY
EDGAR KAUFMANN, JR.

SECOND, REVISED EDITION

DOVER PUBLICATIONS, INC.
NEW YORK

Visiting the House

Fallingwater is a property of the Western Pennsylvania Conservancy. Tours are conducted from April through mid-November every day except Mondays; and from mid-November through March, weather permitting, on Saturdays and Sundays. For further details and ticket reservations, write Fallingwater, Mill Run, Pa. 15464 or call (724) 329-8501.

Copyright © 1978, 1993 by Dover Publications, Inc.

Published in Canada by General Publishing Company, Ltd., 30 Lesmill Road, Don Mills, Toronto, Ontario.

Published in the United Kingdom by Constable and Company, Ltd., 3 The Lanchesters, 162–164 Fulham Palace Road, London W6 9ER.

Frank Lloyd Wright's Fallingwater: The House and Its History/Second, Revised Edition, first published in 1993, is a complete revision of the work originally published by Dover Publications, Inc., in 1978 by special arrangement with the Western Pennsylvania Conservancy, Pittsburgh.

Manufactured in the United States of America
Dover Publications, Inc., 31 East 2nd Street, Mineola, N.Y. 11501

Library of Congress Cataloging-in-Publication Data

Hoffmann, Donald.
    Frank Lloyd Wright's Fallingwater : the house and its history / Donald Hoffmann ; with an introduction by Edgar Kaufmann, Jr. — 2nd rev. ed.
        p.   cm.
    Includes bibliographical references and index.
    ISBN 0-486-27430-6
    1. Wright, Frank Lloyd, 1867–1959. 2. Fallingwater (Pa.) 3. Kaufmann family—Homes and haunts. I. Title.
NA737.W7H6 1993
728'.372'092—dc20
                                                    93-9472
                                                    CIP

Preface to the Second Edition

This book presents a new study grown upon the skeleton of a previous book. My lack of access to the Frank Lloyd Wright Archives severely handicapped the earlier edition, published by Dover Publications in 1978. The documents related to Fallingwater, said Mrs. Wright, could not be made available until the archives were completely catalogued. Memories and hearsay, unfortunately, acquire a specious life of their own as they take further leave from fact; they need to be confronted by documents. And the documents themselves must be brought into close company and compared. Typically, what purports to be a progress report from Bear Run is nothing more than a schedule that could not be met, and a telegram sent by Wright proves to have been misdated by an entire month. In short, the letters and drawings that have now come to light provide the basis for a much expanded and corrected account. They can tell a more coherent, vivid and authentic story of this great work of art. After many more visits to the house, I have also added to my own observations and have changed many of the illustrations and their sequence.

Fallingwater may seem familiar. Nothing about it, however, is obvious. The task as outlined in 1973 by the late Edgar Kaufmann, jr., was to prepare an introductory script for a visitors' center. His own reminiscences, published in Italy in 1962, he considered out-of-date as well as out-of-print. He also said he felt too close to the house, although he was amenable to writing about it for a projected luxury book of color photographs, published finally in 1986. It surprised me in 1973 to find how little was truly known about this very famous building. Although I now dispute certain key points of fact and interpretation published else-where by Edgar Kaufmann, jr., my gratitude for his encouragement and generosity remains undiminished.

This study depended on help from many people. I am indebted most of all to the officers and editors of Dover Publications, Inc., for their unanimous decision to undertake this new edition with new type and many new illustrations. I am also very grateful to my brother John Hoffmann, historian and archivist, for his close critique of the earlier version and for his keen sense of the value of documentary sources. Most of the documents that I have used were graciously provided by Brent Sverdloff of special collections at the Getty Center for the History of Art and the Humanities and by Bruce Brooks Pfeiffer, Indira Berndtson and Oscar Muñoz of the Frank Lloyd Wright Archives. Wright's letters are quoted by permission and are copyright by the Frank Lloyd Wright Foundation, all rights reserved.

For their courtesies at Bear Run, I thank Lynda S. Waggoner, administrator and curator of Fallingwater, and Helene K. Tingle. Ray M. Hall, a grandson of the builder at Bear Run, was exceedingly kind in helping me correct the poor account given of Walter J. Hall in the earlier book. Also most helpful were my son Michael Hoffmann, Harold Corsini, Jack Boucher and Dorothy H. Fickle.

Some of the first Taliesin apprentices have enjoyed long and fruitful lives. It has been my good fortune to correspond regularly with Edgar Tafel and occasionally with Bob Mosher and Jack Howe. The apprentices and others who helped so much with the earlier version of this study were William Wesley Peters, Curtis Besinger, Robert F. Bishop, Robert Warn, Blaine Drake, John Lautner, Abrom Dombar, Mrs. Mendel Glickman, George Nelson, Paul

Grotz, John McAndrew, Lloyd Wright, Robert Mark, Robert Kostka, Brendan Gill, Henry Wright, Adolf K. Placzek, Edward A. Robinson, Earl Friend, Thomas M. Schmidt, Joshua C. Whetzel, jr., Bill Randour, Paul G. Wiegman, Paul L. Cvecko, E. S. Colborn, Oliver M. Kaufmann, my son Alan Hoffmann, J. O. Hedrich, Walter W. Getzel, William E. Edmunds, William R. Upthegrove, Murlin R. Hodgell, Richard Hollander, E. Eugene Young, Roger Kraft, William H. Sims and Gary S. Smith. Many of them, it is saddening to note, are no longer living.

D. H.

Introduction to the First Edition

Fallingwater has provided enjoyment to many people over the years; as a stimulating weekend retreat for the Kaufmann family and their friends, as a source of pride to the architect and his associates, and now—cared for by the Western Pennsylvania Conservancy—as an exceptional experience for visitors from near and far. These varied groups of people have one thing in common, the appreciation of nature. Fallingwater brings people and nature together in an easy relationship; that is the source of its great appeal, of its worldwide fame as one of Frank Lloyd Wright's masterworks. Now, however, country houses so extensive and demanding of services are hardly workable. As a result, has Fallingwater become no more than a delightful relic? No, together with its setting the house illustrates fundamental concepts applicable to different circumstances. The passage of time has brought Fallingwater unanticipated opportunities, and Wright's architecture responds readily.

When Wright came to the site he appreciated the powerful sound of the falls, the vitality of the young forest, the dramatic rock ledges and boulders; these were elements to be interwoven with the serenely soaring spaces of his structure. But Wright's insight penetrated more deeply. He understood that people were creatures of nature, hence an architecture which conformed to nature would conform to what was basic in people. For example, although all of Fallingwater is opened by broad bands of windows, people inside are sheltered as in a deep cave, secure in the sense of hill behind them. Their attention is directed toward the outside by low ceilings; no lordly hall sets the tone but, instead, the luminous textures of the woodland, rhythmically en-framed. The materials of the structure blend with the colorings of rocks and trees, while occasional accents are provided by bright furnishings, like the wildflowers or birds outside. The paths within the house—stairs and passages—meander without formality or urgency, and the house hardly has a main entrance; there are many ways in and out. Sociability and privacy are both available, as are the comforts of home and the adventures of the seasons. So people are cosseted into relaxing, into exploring the enjoyment of a life refreshed in nature. Visitors, too, in due measure experience Wright's architecture as an expansion of living.

The interplay of people and nature does not depend on any one architectural expression, it is a point of view which can be ever freshly manifested. Fallingwater speaks eloquently for this point of view. It indicates a world in which the works of mankind and the processes of nature harmonize productively. Thus it upholds the spirit and purpose of the Western Pennsylvania Conservancy in making nature known as a vital, irreplaceable source of human values.

This book of Donald Hoffmann's, based on his careful research, tells how the house came into being. With delightful fidelity it evokes the volatile but crucial relationship between Wright and my father, and it divulges the complex practicalities of realizing a genial, innovative design. Hoffmann has written a true architectural record, a rare and wonderful accomplishment. Brendan Gill helped unselfishly to make the book a reality. To all concerned with it I express cordial appreciation.

February 1977   EDGAR KAUFMANN, JR.

Contents

List of Illustrations

Frank Lloyd Wright's
FALLINGWATER
The House and Its History

1. Bear Run, Fayette County, Pa.

Bear Run

Of course the stream itself, which is called Bear Run, came first [Fig. 1]. Slight and swift and not very easy to find, Bear Run is fed by mountain springs and it flickers down the western slopes of a ridge called Laurel Hill to join the Youghiogheny River [2]. It moves fast, because in its course of only four miles it falls from about 2500 feet above sea level to about 1070 feet [3]. Bear Run is only a stream, not a town, and it is not well represented on any map of less detail, or lesser scale, than the Mill Run Quadrangle topographic map, as edited and published by the U.S. Geological Survey. Many other runs, or small fast streams, can be found in Stewart Township and in Fayette County, and altogether too many to count in the rest of southwestern Pennsylvania and throughout the Appalachians.

And so Bear Run is both obscure and unexceptional, or so it might have been. But at a place where it flows at 1298 feet above sea level, then breaks to fall about 20 feet, a house was built from plans by Frank Lloyd Wright. He called it "Fallingwater." The owners, who were Mr. and Mrs. Edgar J. Kaufmann of Pittsburgh, more easily thought of their new weekend house simply as "Bear Run," because the place had been their retreat for some 15 years. By whatever name, and from the day in September 1935 when Wright first sketched it, the house was so surely the work of an extraordinary imagination, and so radiant and right for its forest place, it seemed certain to become one of the most celebrated buildings of the twentieth century [4]. And it very soon did.

The house on Bear Run stands today as a remarkable work of art. Many questions can be asked about it. What is the nature of Bear Run? Who was there first, and why? When did the Kaufmanns learn of Bear Run? When did they build their first weekend house? Why did they want a new house? When did they approach Wright? What did Wright notice when he first saw Bear Run? How did he conceive the house? How was it built?

Of the stream itself there is little record, for nature exists so well without man and writes its story, if at all, in no human language. It is far from apparent that in the long period from 600 million to 425 million years ago all of western Pennsylvania was only part of a vast and shallow sea. But geology can tell that much; and also that the crust of the earth, through a tedious contest between the sea and a continental land mass that bordered the southeast corner of Pennsylvania, was layered with sedimentary deposits: the muds, sands and shells that changed so slowly into shales, sandstones and limestones. The strata grew thousands of feet deep, and at first lay almost horizontally. Then some unknown and awesome force within the earth, radiating from the southeast, buckled and arched the rock into parallel open folds. The process began some 230 million years ago. It continued to wrench and twist the rock at an inconceivably slow pace.

Erosion wore down the rock and filled the valleys. Dinosaurs foraged in the swamps until they vanished, about 65 million years ago. About 50 million years ago the plain began to rise; another great force was at work, and it formed the Allegheny Plateau. As the land rose higher, the streams fell farther and flowed faster. They cut deeper channels, opened the valleys and slowly laid bare the ancient folds of rock, mountains older than the Rockies and much older than the Alps.

Bear Run flows into the Ohiopyle Valley, framed by the traces of the ancient mountains, Laurel Hill to the east and

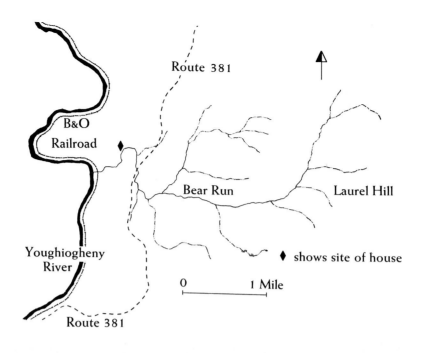

Route 381

B&O
Railroad   ◆

Bear Run   Laurel Hill

◆ shows site of house

Youghiogheny
River

0   1 Mile

Route 381

OPPOSITE, BOTTOM: 2. Mouth of Bear Run. B. & O. tracks at upper left.

OPPOSITE, TOP: 3. Map of Bear Run.

ABOVE: 4. The glen and the house.

5. Morning over Laurel Hill.

Chestnut Ridge to the west [5]. The land near the waterfalls consists of dense and heavy-bedded sandstones of the Pottsville formation, some dark gray, some buff-colored. From weakness came beauty. The stream worked away at a flawed joint in the rock until it fractured; parts of the rock crashed down to rest as huge boulders, and Bear Run broke over falls [6].[1] The falls became central to Wright's conception of the house; the dark boulders on the north side of the stream had much to do with the way in which he sited it, and the buff-colored sandstone ledges that cropped out here and there along the stream offered still another key to its character.

The first Americans in western Pennsylvania were the Indians, who crossed the land to hunt and fish, and left hardly a trace, only a few buried bones and artifacts. British troops in the later 1750s reported signs of Indians a few miles north of the Bear Run falls. The Indians that passed through the valley were from the Delaware, Shawnee and Iroquois peoples, and they called it "Ohiopehelle," meaning a white-water place, just as they named the river the "Yohoghany," in description of its twisted course north to the Monongahela. White settlers reached the valley slowly, toward the end of the eighteenth century. Most were of English, German and Irish Protestant origins. Gradually they gathered into a small community three and a half miles north of the falls; at first it was called Bigamtown, but since 1866 it has been known as Mill Run because of Reuben Skinner's gristmill.[2] Milling lasted in the valley until the 1940s, but was not among the principal ways by which the mountain people lived off the land—rarely to the land's advantage, often enough not even to their own. Mining was important and so was timbering. Coal and clay were taken from the hills, and on the Bear Run grounds even the sandstone was broken up to be sold as "ganister rock," for use in making brick kilns or refractory products such as silica brick; in 1920, the rock was bringing 25 cents a ton. The forest was cut over, again and again, for posts and mining

[1]The typical rock-structure pattern in Stewart Township is illustrated in W. O. Hickok IV and F. T. Moyer, *Geology and Mineral Resources of Fayette County Pennsylvania* (Harrisburg, Pa., 1940), fig. 113, although the relation of the rock beds is now thought to be more complex, with interbeddings from different ages. Also see Bradford Willard, *Pennsylvania Geology Summarized* (Harrisburg, Pa., 1962).

[2]See *A History of Mill Run, Fayette County, Pennsylvania* (Mill Run, Pa., 1970) and Solon Justus Buck and Elizabeth Hawthorn Buck, *The Planting of Civilization in Western Pennsylvania* (Pittsburgh, Pa., 1939).

timbers and railroad ties. Tramways crossed the grounds to convey the timbers to the Youghiogheny, where a sawmill stood on a site of more than five acres near the mouth of Bear Run. And there was a pulp mill a few miles up the river, at the village of Ohiopyle.

When the first members of the Kaufmann family arrived in western Pennsylvania well before the turn of the century and picked their way through the sparsely settled mountains to sell cloths and notions, they often encountered trappers; and as late as 1933 a game commissioner could report that fox, mink, weasel and skunk were still being trapped along Bear Run. The stream was fished with a certain biblical devotion: One man boasted in 1880 of having caught 153 trout in a single day's work (the exact number of fish given in John 21:11). Some chose to be farmers, although the forest and rocks gave them little encouragement; as if in revenge for the unyielding nature of the soil, they cared very little about erosion. The mountain people tended to live a frontier life long after the American Frontier as an epoch of history had ended. If today Bear Run looks unspoiled, it is not because the land and the timber are in any sense virgin. Nature with help has healed some of the lesser wounds, and the dense forest cover conceals most of the evidence of what man has done to the land.

Bear Run revels in its native plant life. Most characteristic is the great laurel, or common rhododendron, which can flourish from the moisture of the stream, the shade of the taller trees and a soil enriched by fallen oak leaves. In every season the long smooth leaves stay green, and in summertime the white blossoms ornament the forest with a fragile beauty [7]. Mountain laurels are intermixed, and so are the oaks and other hardwoods and the little Christmas ferns that descend from the giant ferns of the ancient era when the coal beds were formed. The trees near the waterfalls when Wright first saw Bear Run included white oak, black oak, red oak, birch, tulip, maple, hickory, butternut, apple and wild black cherry.[3]

No one showed much care about Bear Run until 1890, when a group of Masons from Pittsburgh bought more than 135 acres from Joseph Soisson, Zachariah Moon and a few other settlers. Not that the Masons were conservationists, but at least they saw in Bear Run a recreational value. They built a "Masonic Country Club," and in August 1895 bought about 1500 acres more. But within a decade the club had failed. The property was sold at a sheriff's auction in June 1906, sold again in October 1907 and still again in March 1909, when another Masonic body from Pittsburgh, the Syria Improvement Association, acquired the camp and

[3]As identified by a contour map of March 9, 1935. John F. Lewis, in his *Guide to Plants, Bear Run Nature Reserve* (Pittsburgh, Pa., 1968), identified 501 species, and Frank L. Lowden has found 33 more. In recent years about 130 kinds of birds have been sighted, and more than 20 mammals, ranging from the tiny woodland jumping mouse to the northern white-tailed deer. Black bears have at last returned.

6. The waterfalls, before 1912.

7. Rhododendron at Bear Run.

8. Syria Country Club House, before 1912.

revived it as the "Syria Country Club."[4] By then there were more than a dozen buildings: six cottages, various outbuildings, a dance pavilion and the clubhouse [8].

It was also in 1909 that Edgar Jonas Kaufmann married Lillian Sarah Kaufmann.[5] They married in New York City because they could not do so in Pennsylvania; they were first cousins. Kaufmann was the elder son of Morris Kaufmann, and his bride was the daughter of Isaac Kaufmann. Morris and Isaac and two more brothers of theirs, Henry and Jacob, had left Viernheim, in Hessen, Germany, and arrived in western Pennsylvania in the 1860s. They were tailors and merchants, and very good ones. In 1871, with only $1500, they opened a store in Pittsburgh, mostly to offer ready-made men's clothing. The business grew, they moved in 1885 to a building at Fifth Avenue and Smithfield Street, and there Kaufmann's Store has stayed ever since.

Edgar J. Kaufmann was born in 1885, and he grew along with the business. He trained in Germany, in Marshall Field's in Chicago and in a general store in Connellsville, only 16 miles from Bear Run. By 1913, when his father bought Henry Kaufmann's interest in the store and he bought Isaac's—Jacob had died in 1905—Edgar J. Kaufmann took active control of Kaufmann's Store. Among his papers is a plan of the Bear Run property dated November 1913.[6] It shows the Syria Club House about

1100 feet southeast of the falls, and it also shows a Bear Run Station on the Baltimore & Ohio Railroad, high above the mouth of the stream; access to the club grounds from Pittsburgh to a large extent depended on the railroad and the willingness of the engineers to stop on a steep uphill grade. Thirteen other structures—all of them now gone—are shown on the map. One, identified as the Porter cottage, is on the cliff north of the falls, where Kaufmann was to build the servants' wing of Fallingwater so many years later [9]. The road to the Porter cottage crosses a simple wooden truss bridge east of the falls. Nearby, a hatchery for brook trout provides evidence enough that the native supply already was exhausted.

It is not clear whether the plan of 1913, prepared by William Bradford, a Pittsburgh engineer, was drawn at Kaufmann's request. But in 1916 he established "Kaufmann's Summer Club" at Bear Run as a vacation spot for women employees of the store.[7] A brochure from 1926 describes the activities: tennis, swimming, hiking, volleyball, hayrides, picnicking, sunbathing, theater, singing and "quiet" reading. A retreat from "the heat and turmoil of the city," the club was 72 miles from Pittsburgh, a

[4]The chain of title can be traced in deed books 137–139, 146, 261, 291, 321, 379, 406, 471, 472, 519, 535 and 982, Fayette County Recorder of Deeds, Uniontown, Pa.

[5]She later changed the spelling of her name to "Liliane."

[6]His papers relating to Bear Run and Wright are in the Avery Architectural Library of Columbia University, New York.

[7]Kaufmann may have learned of Bear Run through Charles A. Filson, a store detective, close friend and Mason. Filson was an advisory director of the summer club, and occasionally represented Kaufmann in club matters. The club was run by the Kaufmann Beneficial and Protective Association, an employees' organization. The store in those years also had a social-service department; a paternalistic concern for working women was typical of the time. The landscape architect Jens Jensen expressed it as late as 1929: "What do our young people, spending their lives in great buildings, have in their heads? . . . Little except sex! Trees and water and sky have things to tell them which they should hear if their minds are not to become narrow . . ." (*Chicago Daily News*, June 24, 1929, sec. 2, p. 14).

train ride of only two hours. The station was the starting point for a climb "up the mountain road lined with mountain laurel and rhododendron to the accompaniment of the gentle roar of the water in Bear Run . . . ." (The road leading up to the camp was on the south side of the stream and is still kept clear. The station stood at an elevation 260 feet lower than that of the clubhouse. Edgar Kaufmann, jr., remembered it simply as an old freight car with one side removed; an early photograph shows it to have been well disguised.)

In the years when Kaufmann's Summer Club leased the camp at Bear Run, the property changed hands again. More than 600 acres were sold in December 1918 for only $20,000. Early in 1920, Kaufmann was offered 300 acres, including all the improvements, at $25,000. He considered the property cautiously and with a great deal of foresight. He asked Morris Knowles, Inc., a Pittsburgh firm of engineers, to report on the entire site—the topography, water, sewerage and mineral resources. In a report of March 24, 1920, they estimated the value of the improvements alone at $48,000; but by then only 130 acres were offered for sale.

The engineers in June presented a general plan to develop the summer camp. They recommended that Kaufmann buy the entire grounds, especially to prevent contamination of the watershed by coal-mine openings, lumber camps and trespassers.

The negotiations came to nothing, but for the first time there was a clear understanding of the need to conserve Bear Run by gaining control of the watershed. Some of the camp buildings were remodeled and repaired for the 1920 season, and in 1921 the club took a second five-year lease. That same year, Kaufmann and his wife built their first weekend house on Bear Run, a modest "Readi-cut" summer cabin from the Aladdin Company of Bay City, Michigan.[8] They built the Aladdin cabin about 1500 feet southeast of the falls, slightly west of the road between Mill Run and Ohiopyle, and at the edge of a cliff; soon everyone began calling the cabin the "Hangover." It had screened

[8]The company's *Catalog No. 32* (Bay City, 1919–20), p. 3, asserts that "every bit of work that *can* be done by machine *should* be so done," and compares the Readi-cut system with the fabrication of steel for skyscrapers.

9. Porter cottage and wooden bridge near falls, before 1912.

porches on every side, but was without plumbing, heating or electricity. In May 1926 the store employees' association bought the Bear Run property: 1598.07 acres. Kaufmann held the mortgage. Gradually, the summer camp lost its appeal; once, because of labor troubles, it was boycotted. With the Depression, the place fell into disuse. Kaufmann nonetheless continued to regard Bear Run with great affection.

When he was advised in 1932 by V. M. Bearer, the district forester, to remove as soon as possible the "old dead chestnuts"—victims of the 1920s chestnut blight—Kaufmann made a note to have them made into split-rail fences, as well as firewood. He also had a few trunks sawed into rustic cocktail tables. Bearer suggested that the care-taker, Herbert Ohler, might well plant a few thousand Norway spruce trees in the openings of the forest. Kaufmann had that done too, and he must have been pleased when W. L. Wright of the International Association of Game, Fish and Conservation Commissioners wrote in February 1933, praising the grounds as "one of the best ranges for a game preserve that I have ever looked over." He corresponded in May with the Pennsylvania Board of Fish Commissioners about a plan to replenish the brook trout in Bear Run.

By the time Kaufmann and his wife took title to the grounds personally, in July 1933, they were committed to a comprehensive program of conservation. They eventually owned 1914 acres on Bear Run.

The House Is Conceived
1934–35

In 1934 there was good reason to assume that Frank Lloyd Wright was well into the twilight years of his long and immensely productive career. He turned 67 years old that June, and although his home "Taliesin," south of Spring Green, Wisconsin, was alive with eager apprentices, his architectural practice had shriveled to almost nothing. In the summer of 1932 he planned a house for Malcolm Willey, in Minneapolis. More than a year and a half later he was still at work on drawings of a second scheme for the same house; and it was not by any means a large house. The first version would have cost $16,500, Wright estimated, and the house as built in 1934 cost $10,000. But of course these were the Depression years. Even so, the house for Willey was only the second commission that Wright had seen realized since 1927, and the first was a house for his cousin, Richard Lloyd Jones. Wright was never not busy, as one of his apprentices, Bob Mosher, has remarked; but at the time—so far as the world outside Taliesin could tell—he was up to very little beyond his writing and lecturing. A sense of frustration appeared even in the way he used words: "I would much rather build than write about building," he wrote in 1928, "but when I am not building, I will write about building—or the significance of those buildings I have already built."[1]

From those lean years came *An Autobiography*, the long and episodic narrative in which Wright revealed his emotional depth even more forcefully than the radical nature of his architecture. It was first published in the spring of 1932, and a few months later Wright and his wife Olgivanna announced that they planned to accept apprentices-in-resi-

dence, beginning in October. They named their program the Taliesin Fellowship. Robert F. Bishop, who meant to make only a short visit to Taliesin in the summer of 1932, but stayed nearly three years, has described the Fellowship as a studio-workshop situation "somewhat akin to the studio-workshops of the Renaissance, but with a collective farm thrown in."[2] Originally, there were about 35 apprentices and assistants, and whether or not they paid "tuition," they gained no academic credit whatsoever. They did learn, soon enough, that they would be obliged to perform tasks that seemed to have little to do with their training as architects: Besides sawing oak, quarrying sandstone and operating a lime kiln to furnish the materials for continual remodelings and extensions of the Taliesin buildings, they grew vegetables, cooked, served, washed dishes and cleaned house. "Outside of the Studio," Edgar Tafel has recalled of the winters of 1932 and 1933, "we kept in trim by going off to the woods every other day to fell trees as fuel for the boilers and fireplaces. Half of the Fellowship was keeping the other half warm."[3] Such experiences could not be forgotten. Despite the menial labor, few apprentices regretted their stay at Taliesin, and many regarded their months or years with Wright as the best time of their lives.

An Autobiography affected many people in many ways. Edgar Kaufmann, jr., was 24 years old and back from a long stay in Europe when, in mid-1934, a friend who worked in a New York art gallery expressed her great enthusiasm for Wright's book. He soon read it with a deep

---

[1]Wright, "In the Cause of Architecture—The Terms," *Architectural Record*, 64 (Dec. 1928), p. 512.

[2]Letter of June 21, 1974.

[3]*Prairie School Review*, V (4th quarter, 1968), p. 27. Also see Tafel's memoir, *Years with Frank Lloyd Wright: Apprentice to Genius* (Dover: New York, 1985).

sense of personal discovery. "I had no inkling of the character of his art, and his story flowed into my mind like the first trickle of irrigation in a desert land," he wrote nearly 30 years later.[4] He talked with his parents about Wright, and his father soon approached Wright about some civic projects in Pittsburgh. "I would greatly appreciate hearing from you, or your secretary, whether or not you ever visit Pittsburgh or New York City," the elder Kaufmann wrote on August 16.

Wright usually sensed a potential client very quickly, particularly one of great wealth; but now he took a month to respond. He wrote Kaufmann on September 18 that he could not afford to travel East at his own expense:

> As you know, there has been no building to speak of these past years and architects, good and bad, have been severely hit by the Depression for this reason, to say the least. Probably wiped out.
>
> Could I do anything for you by correspondence?[5]

Although he had no plans to become an architect, Edgar Kaufmann, jr., traveled to Taliesin for an interview on September 27 as a candidate for the Fellowship. At last Wright learned that the elder Kaufmann was a man he should not neglect. He wrote the next day:

> I was interested long ago in the planetarium as an architect's problem—and would like to do one to your satisfaction.
>
> Your son Edgar is a fine chap and we look forward with pleasure to having him here with us. I hope you and Mrs. Kaufmann can come here to visit us someday.[6]

Five days later, Wright asked Eugene Masselink, who served as his secretary, to send Kaufmann *The Life-Work of the American Architect Frank Lloyd Wright,* a sumptuous volume published in Holland in 1925 (reprinted by Dover Publications as *Frank Lloyd Wright: The Complete 1925 Wendingen Series).*

Edgar Kaufmann, jr., joined the Fellowship on October 15, and on November 16 his parents arrived for a visit. At

10. Edgar J. Kaufmann in his office.

49, E. J. Kaufmann was an exceptionally successful businessman, and by all accounts was just as his son has described him, "a magnetic and unconventional person." He loved to build things, and he possessed every quality that Wright admired in a client [10]. "Mr. Wright and Mr. Kaufmann had great rapport from the start, each with genuine admiration for the other," John H. Howe, one of Wright's chief lieutenants, has recalled.[7] Nearly a year later, when Kaufmann introduced Wright as a speaker to The Hungry Club, in Pittsburgh, he would say that:

> although Mr. Wright has always faced the severest opposition from officialdom—public and professional—there has rarely been a moment during his long career when he has not found an appreciative client among a group of open-minded, sincere American business men and women who realized from their own experience the value, or at least part of it, of what he had to give them in spite of the lack of seals and red tape around his reputation.

[4]"Twenty-five Years of the House on the Waterfall," *L'architettura—cronache e storia,* 82 (Aug. 1962), p. 39. After attending the Shady Side Academy in Pittsburgh from 1924 to 1927, the younger Kaufmann studied painting in New York, in Vienna at the Kunstgewerbeschule and in London and Florence with Victor Hammer.

[5]The elder Kaufmann may have been aware of Wright through the Pittsburgh architect Benno Janssen (1874–1964), who knew such prominent stage and industrial designers as Norman Bel Geddes, Joseph Urban and Paul T. Frankl—all of whom knew Wright. Janssen and his partner W. Y. Cocken had designed the picturesque house the Kaufmanns built in 1924–25 in the Fox Chapel borough of Pittsburgh, and they also redesigned the ground floor of Kaufmann's Store in an Art Deco mode; it reopened in May 1930.

[6]The first planetarium was opened in Munich in 1924; in 1925, Wright proposed a grand planetarium inside the "automobile objective" he designed for Sugarloaf Mountain, Md., the property of a Chicago real-estate entrepreneur named Gordon Strong (1869–1954). The project came to nothing. See Mark Reinberger, "The Sugarloaf Mountain Project and Frank Lloyd Wright's Vision of a New World," *Journal of the Society of Architectural Historians (JSAH)* XLIII (March 1984), pp. 38–52.

[7]Letter of Dec. 31, 1973. Wright frequently expressed his appreciation for adventurous American businessmen as clients. In *An Autobiography* (all citations will be to the revised edition, New York, 1943), p. 448, he described Kaufmann as "a good business man as well as a good fellow too."

When they first met, Kaufmann and Wright talked about Pittsburgh and the possibility of building a planetarium. They also talked about "Broadacre City," or Wright's vision of a prototype American community. *The Disappearing City,* a book he published in the fall of 1932, had met with little success, and not without reason. The text was as vague as it was brief, and the few illustrations—there were only six—gave no clear idea of his ideal city. Broadacre City cried out for expression in plans and models. Now came the chance. Wright learned of a New York exposition in which he might exhibit, and he put the apprentices to work on a large model, 12 feet square. He telegraphed Kaufmann on December 3 that he needed $500 for work on the model to continue. The next day Kaufmann sent the money. Kaufmann also wrote optimistically about the public works prospects in Pittsburgh, and said "it is time for you to appear on the scene." Wright finally began to plan a trip East. He wrote Kaufmann on December 7 that he had just received a floor plan of the exposition and was dismayed to find only a meager space assigned to Broadacre City:

Evidently the importance of the Broadacre, its virtuosity and beauty, have been sidetracked for a transportation show of no great significance so far as architecture is concerned, as I see the layout.

But with your permission we will just go on with our model and have a significant show of our own somewhere in good times. I can't understand these people after the representations made to me . . . I hope you will concur with me that something better worthwhile will eventually come out of our joint effort.

For the most significant constructive thing of our modern times to be shut off, or in, by a couple of automobiles and a train model is characteristic enough but I was given to understand this was to be *different* throughout.

Sincerely sorry but with you just the same—as I hope you are with me.

Wright took the train to Pittsburgh and met with Kaufmann on December 18. One of the projects they discussed was a new office for Kaufmann on the top floor of the department store.

Then they went down to Bear Run. Kaufmann and his wife had been thinking about a new weekend house. The road below the cliff where the Aladdin cabin stood (now Pennsylvania Route 381) had been paved in 1930, and each year seemed to bring more traffic, noise and fumes—especially on Saturday nights. The cabin could hardly qualify as a country retreat. What the Kaufmanns had in mind was a year-round weekend house, with the modern conveniences, away from the highway and closer to the waterfalls, where they most liked to go for sunning, bathing and picnicking.

Wright looked at the stream, the falls, the trees, the rock ledges, the boulders and rhododendron. He already had said what rock meant to him:

The rock-ledges of a stone-quarry are a story and a longing to me. There is suggestion in the strata and character in the formations. I like to sit and feel it, as it is. Often I have thought, were great monumental buildings ever given me to build, I would go to the Grand Canyon of Arizona to ponder them . . . For in the stony bone-work of the Earth, the principles that shaped stone as it lies, or as it rises and remains to be sculptured by winds and tide—there sleep forms and styles enough for all the ages for all of Man.[8]

Wright told Kaufmann to send him a contour map that would locate every boulder and every large tree. After he left Bear Run he went on to New York, where he negotiated better space for Broadacre City—"the center of the stage," he told Kaufmann later. He took a fast train back West with his friend Alexander Woollcott, the writer. The day after Christmas 1934 he wrote Kaufmann about his delight with Bear Run:

The visit to the waterfall in the woods stays with me and a domicile has taken vague shape in my mind to the music of the stream. When contours come you will see it. Meantime, to you my affection.

Kaufmann had become more than a client. He was a patron. Except for a projected house for Stanley Marcus, nearly every prospect the Fellowship saw for 1935 was connected with Kaufmann: the office, the weekend house, the planetarium and the models of Broadacre City.[9] In a letter of January 10, 1935, Wright asked Kaufmann for another $250 to help with the Broadacre City models; he also inquired about the contour map of Bear Run. Kaufmann and his wife left Pittsburgh on February 14 for a vacation in the West. For some reason—bad weather, perhaps—the topographic map still had not been made. A memorandum of February 20 in the files of Morris Knowles, Engineers, notes the need to furnish a "plane table survey" very quickly: "Mr. Kaufmann wishes particularly to identify the larger trees and the character of the rock outcrops . . . Mr. Kaufmann is particularly anxious to have the survey cleaned up this week as he is thinking of building a house at the camp in the spring." The map was finished March 9 [11].

It noted every tree of six or more inches in diameter, and stated that the rock outcrops and boulders were of a hard sandstone. Only a small area was embraced—the scale was one inch to 20 feet—and the wooden truss bridge a short distance east of the falls appeared at the upper righthand

[8]Wright, "In the Cause of Architecture: The Meaning of Materials—Stone," *Architectural Record,* 63 (Apr. 1928), pp. 350, 356.

[9]The house for Marcus was never built. Mr. and Mrs. Paul Hanna discussed a house with Wright in June 1935, long before they had a site in Palo Alto, Calif. He sent the first sketches for their hexagram or "Honeycomb" house in Apr. 1936, a few months before they acquired a site.

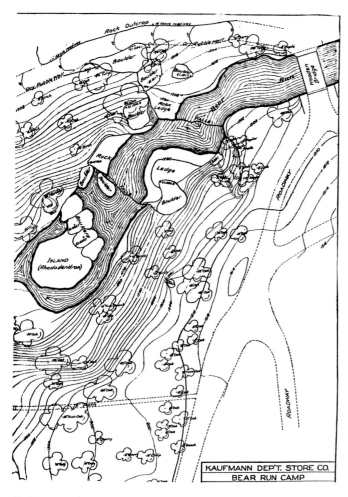

11. Topographic map of building site, March 1935.

Broadacre City was due to go on exhibit April 15 in New York. "The trip was *literally* 'en charrette,' the meaning of which you will appreciate if you know the Parisian Beaux-Arts origin of the term," Robert F. Bishop has recalled, referring to students who had to compete against strict deadlines and thus hastened to get their projects on the passing charrette, a cart for collecting the drawings. "We started late, allowed just enough time to make the grand opening, then ran into and through the worst dust-storm on record, clear across the lengthy state of Kansas." Bishop was traveling with Edgar Tafel, Bob Mosher and Edgar Kaufmann, jr. They took turns driving a small car that belonged to Kaufmann and a truck that carried the models and announced itself as Wright's emissary by its color, red, and its Taliesin insigne, a tight linear pattern within a square. The square, to Wright, "potently" suggested integrity. Red, his favorite color, likewise was symbolic. "The color red is invincible," he quoted Timiriazev, the plant physiologist, as saying. "It is the color not only of the blood—it is the color of creation. It is the only life-giving color in nature filling the sprouting plant with life and giving warmth to everything in creation . . . ."[10]

When the models got to the Industrial Arts Exposition in the Forum of Rockefeller Center, they were installed under Wright's banner proclaiming "A New Freedom." Wright himself arrived in time for the opening; he was to be one of the speakers. "As everyone knows, we live in economic, aesthetic and moral chaos," he said, "for the reason that American life has achieved no organic form." An architect "should at least see life as organic form continually," Wright emphasized. After the trip to the New York exposition, Bishop and Edgar Kaufmann, jr., left the Fellowship. "Bob Mosher and I manned the show," Tafel has recalled, "and Mr. Wright was staying at the Lafayette Hotel. We all took a trip to Southampton with a possible client. Actually, Mr. Wright was trying to look for publicity and new clients through the exhibition."[11]

So far as publicity, Wright did well. His speech was reported in the *Times,* and Broadacre City got good notice in *The New Yorker* and in both the *Architectural Record* and the *American Architect.*[12] In New York, the notion of a planned

corner. The rest of the map reached west and south past the falls. From the area surveyed, it could be surmised that Kaufmann envisioned the house downstream from the falls; whatever had assumed "vague shape" in Wright's mind was resting there in secrecy.

Kaufmann and his wife hoped to stay near Wright's desert camp at Chandler, Arizona, where the apprentices continued to work on Broadacre City, but Wright could not secure accommodations. He wrote Kaufmann at Palm Springs, California, on March 8:

We all have a sense of calamity befallen because you are not here with us although I know Palm Springs is a delightful place . . .

Junior is sagging a little. He feels his end here with us is near, for which I am deeply sorry. Just as we were getting attached to him he is off somewhere, but if it is to you it is not so bad. His time here has not been wasted. He has been a fine spirit and a good worker. No doubt you need him and he will be a great help and comfort to you . . .

The model [of Broadacre City] is now emerging from chaos. I am sure it is going to do us all proud . . . .

[10]*Architectural Forum,* 68 (Jan. 1938), fol. p. 102. Kliment Arkadevich Timiriazev (1843–1920) was best known in this country as the author of *The Life of the Plant,* already in its seventh revised edition by 1912. Wright's insigne somehow managed to be different from any of the 3064 designs in Flinders Petrie, *Decorative Patterns of the Ancient World* (London, 1930; Dover reprint, 1974), although Petrie no doubt would have associated it with the "complex key patterns."

[11]Letter of July 29, 1974. Tafel has continued to correspond since 1974, and has furnished much further information.

[12]*New York Times,* Apr. 16, 1935, p. 23; Lewis Mumford, "The Sky Line," *The New Yorker,* 11 (Apr. 27, 1935), pp. 79–80; *Architectural Record,* 77 (Apr. 1935), pp. 243–254, and *American Architect,* 146 (May 1935), pp. 55–62. Mumford found Broadacre City to be "both a generous dream and a rational plan"; many years later, however, he wrote that it "made every social activity call for long distance transportation and therefore the incessant use of the motor car," and was merely a coherent pattern for the random forces that disintegrated the American city. See *Architectural Record,* 132 (Dec. 1962), p. 102.

community based on a minimum of one acre for the child-less couple, more space for the larger family and a motorcar for every citizen must have seemed pure fantasy. Wright nevertheless quite accurately presented the models as an interpretation of the tendencies in American growth; the census of 1970 found more people living in suburbs than in cities. So central to Broadacre City was the motorcar that some of the collateral models meant to illustrate types of dwellings were identified by the number of cars they harbored. The "two-car" residence had features that would appear more forcefully in the house on Bear Run: a broad cantilevered terrace and a flat roof slab perforated to form a horizontal trellis, or arbor.

Wright found no chance to talk privately with E. J. Kaufmann in New York, but he wrote him from Taliesin on April 27, saying that he was "ready to go to work on the waterfall cottage at Bear Run and the Planetarium." The trouble, he wrote, was a perennial lack of funds. By then, Kaufmann already had contributed $1000 for the Broadacre City project; but Wright had no qualms in asking him for a $15,000 loan to be secured by 40 Japanese prints that Wright himself appraised as "worth at least $4800." Kaufmann was generous, but not a fool. He wrote Wright on May 4:

I too find myself in a position where I have to be careful as to how to balance my budget for the next few years, in fact I am not balancing it—but trying to keep from going too far into the red . . .

I have a deep feeling for the situation in which you find yourself and I have tried in a modest way to go along with you. I would ask you, therefore, to cast elsewhere to help you out at this particular time.

A few days ago Junior entered the business. He is now going through what is known as our Junior Executive Training Course. As he made this decision of his own free will I am hoping he will not regret it. From my point of view naturally it is most welcome, provided he is happy. He will be a great help to me in years to come.

Wright responded on May 12:

I recognize the limitations . . . In the circumstances, how do you feel about going on with plans for Bear Run, the Planetarium and the office?

We are ready if you are still of a mind to go after them. I am glad Junior is settling . . . My best to you all—we will manage somehow as we always have managed to go along.

He already had coaxed some money from Edgar Kaufmann, jr. On May 22 the elder Kaufmann wrote Wright:

I am interested in your making sketches for our consideration of both the office and the house at Bear Run, but before starting I should like to know how much you estimate each of these would cost in preliminary sketch. This would at

least keep these situations alive until estimates could be gotten at some future time, to see whether or not we care to go ahead.

In the meantime, Kaufmann was arranging to exhibit Broadacre City in Pittsburgh. Wright soon distorted this favor into an obligation, and another opportunity to plead for money. He wrote Kaufmann on June 15 that several tired apprentices had left Taliesin with the models the night before, headed toward Pittsburgh:

I hope the show is a success because I find it a hell of a lot of trouble and expense continually to keep it up. It takes young people away from here when we need them most . . . I've no doubt with the models here we could collect fifty or a hundred dollars a week this summer with no expense or much trouble at all.

You however are entitled to the showing beyond anyone else, although some talk reached me that you had changed your original interest and now expected to be reimbursed for your "grub-stake" so generously offered . . . if you do feel that way about it—contrary as it is to the statement you made at the time and on which I accepted your help, we will try to arrange some way to pay back the money to you gradually.

For instance, we are laying out your office and furniture now for which work we make a charge of 20% usually. We are starting on the Home at "Bear Run," a specially difficult project, but on which we will charge you the usual ten percent fee only. We will allow something out of these fees . . .

You will see some drawings from us soon. Meantime, look after the orphans a little, will you?

Nine days later he sent Kaufmann a bill for "model rental and expenses."

The "orphans" who took the models to Pittsburgh were Blaine Drake, Abe Dombar and Cornelia Brierly. Broadacre City there became part of an exposition titled "New Homes for Old." It was sponsored by the Federal Housing Administration, and it opened June 18 on the eleventh floor of Kaufmann's Store. Edgar Kaufmann, jr., helped interpret the models, and soon sent Wright a report:

I should have written before this, to thank you for the opportunity of working in connection with Broadacres . . . People keep crowding in—we've had an easy average of 1,000 a day, with only moderate advertising and publicity—and most of them are very anxious to listen to a verbal explanation . . . At least six people have asked how to get in touch with you for plans, so I gave them your address altho' they were usually engineers, commercial artists or other technicians with not more than 3–5,000 dollars to spend on a house.

It looked like fine work for the Fellowship, at least. The family has talked more about the office and house than anything else, since you wrote. They are going to be wonderful events for us; but I cannot help thinking how very many small houses of your design must be really wanted all over the country . . .

I have not forgotten what you told me the night before I left, and realize its truth. Still, out of myself, I know that I can only improve by my own unaided powers, if at all. I am not good material for your real needs; but I hope always to fulfill the less enviable role of sincere, and I trust a little useful, propagandist.

Wright missed the opening of the exposition in Pittsburgh, but introduced himself by writing in the *Sun-Telegraph*. "The principle Allegheny County seems to have put to work is 'to hell with nature, and we'll get what we want in spite of her,' " he wrote, offending an editorialist, who hastened to call him a "dreamer," and also the mayor, William N. McNair, who objected that Broadacre City was utopian, paternalistic and socialistic. Wright's ideas about city planning represented a natural extension of his ideas about individual dwellings, or dwellings for individuals, and while writing about Pittsburgh he was evidently thinking about Bear Run:

Well—at this late day it isn't good medicine, perhaps, to imagine (now) how the river might have been made into a beautiful feature by damming and pooling it into placid water and driving across the broad dams to the tune of waterfalls, into and up to broad terraced levels picturesquely related to the water . . . .[13]

When he arrived in Pittsburgh, and was taken on a tour of the city on June 29—it was the last day of the exposition and the last day of the store's 64th anniversary sale—Wright made sarcastic comments about everything except the Court House and County Jail, great stone buildings he already knew as the work of H. H. Richardson, one of the few American architects for whom he professed any respect at all. The tour ended with the model residential community of Chatham Village, where the Buhl Foundation had just announced plans to build 68 more brick row houses. "It's a great way to sell bricks," Wright was said to have remarked. Finally, when someone asked how he would rebuild Pittsburgh, he answered: "It would be cheaper to abandon it . . . ."[14]

One of the apprentices sent to Pittsburgh with the models, Blaine Drake, has recalled that he drove Wright to Bear Run that summer. He was not aware that Wright had been there the previous December:

He never mentioned that to me . . . and it was his nature to talk freely most of the time when we were driving. Perhaps his having been there explains why he was able to describe so

completely his concept of the ultimate design, as he usually wasn't in a hurry to begin a new design . . . The finished design was as I visualized it when he was talking to the Kaufmanns. I remember E. J. being quite surprised that the house would be above the falls. He told F. Ll. W. he had always expected the house to be on the opposite side of the Run, looking at the falls from below . . . .[15]

Kaufmann wrote on July 5 to confirm the fee schedule he had discussed with Wright: 10 percent of the cost of installing the office, 20 percent on the furniture and 10 percent on the house at Bear Run. He had mailed Wright a blueprint of the office space on December 21, and he expected the office to be done first; his enthusiasm was tempered only slightly by his increasing familiarity with Wright's cavalier regard for money:

When proceeding with the preliminary sketches and floor plans for the Bear Run home, we should have in mind that the total cost of construction plus the furnishings should be between $20,000 and $30,000. I would prefer if you would start making the layout keeping in mind the $20,000 figure because we both agreed that in the process of building and completion there will be some additions which will always creep in to make the cost more than $20,000. So let us aim at that figure and see what might be produced . . . I hope you will proceed with the office as quickly as possible as I really should like to have it constructed during the summer months so that I might occupy it in September.

Weeks went by without word from Wright about the office plans. "Will you let me know whether or not you have started," Kaufmann asked on August 12, "and, if not, is there any reason why you are not going ahead?" Wright performed always at his own pace. "We're working," he answered on August 21. "You'll have some results soon." Of course he had said the same thing two months earlier. Edgar Kaufmann, jr., grew anxious too; he wrote Wright how delighted everyone had been when Edgar Tafel sent a note that said the office and house were both to some extent "on paper." To what extent, however, remained a mystery; Wright avoided the drafting board even after the elder Kaufmann on August 22 sent him a $250 retainer for sketches of the house. "He had the design totally in his head, as always," John Lautner has recalled, "and as he recommended to the apprentices, if no whole idea, no architecture."[16] A few years earlier, Wright had described his procedure:

conceive the building in the imagination, not on paper but in the mind, thoroughly—before touching paper. Let it live

[13]Wright, "Broadacres to Pittsburgh," *Pittsburgh Sun-Telegraph,* June 24, 1935, ed. page. In *Taliesin,* 1 (Oct. 1940), Wright published a revised version of his article, as well as his speech at the New York exposition.

[14]James A. Baubie, "Flings Sneers at Pittsburgh," *Sun-Telegraph,* June 30, 1935, part I, p. 13. Chatham Village has been considered one of the most successfully designed housing projects in the country; see Norman T. Newton, *Design on the Land* (Cambridge, Mass., 1971), pp. 496–500. Wright's comment about abandoning Pittsburgh has been widely quoted ever since he made it.

[15]Letter of May 19, 1975. Drake joined the fellowship in January 1933 and stayed until the summer of 1941. Other apprentices recall Kaufmann having no idea of the house until he saw the first sketches. J. F. Kienitz, in "The Romanticism of Frank Lloyd Wright," *Art in America,* 32 (Apr. 1944), pp. 99–101, wrote that Wright saw Bear Run only once before Kaufmann's visit to Taliesin forced him to make the first sketches.

[16]Letter of June 20, 1974. Lautner was an apprentice from 1933 to 1939.

there—gradually taking more definite form before committing it to the draughting board. When the thing lives for you—start to plan it with tools. Not before . . . Working on it with triangle and T square should modify or extend or intensify or test the conception—complete the harmonious adjustment of its parts.[17]

He probably would have waited even longer if he had not heard by August 26 that Kaufmann and Irwin D. Wolf, who was vice president of the store, were to be in Milwaukee for a meeting of the Cavendish consortium of retailers, and planned to drive to Taliesin afterward, on September 22.

About that Sunday at Taliesin, when Wright appears to have made his first definite drawings for Fallingwater, there are various and conflicting accounts: After so many years, the memory can play strange tricks. John Lautner recalls Wright working from the topographic map and getting his ideas down on tracing paper within 15 or 20 minutes. Blaine Drake thinks Wright began the sketches immediately after they returned from Bear Run, earlier that summer, and chose to work in private. "He usually enjoyed an audience while he was working," Drake has recalled. "This was his way of teaching. But this day he said, 'Boys, I would like to work on this alone.' " Cornelia Brierly has recalled that Wright made the sketches so early in the morning that the apprentices were surprised to see them already on his drafting table as they passed through the studio on their way to breakfast, at 6:30.

The apprentices who became the most intimately involved with the house on Bear Run were Bob Mosher and Edgar Tafel. Mosher could recall Wright beginning to work only after getting a telephone call from Kaufmann, who was just leaving Milwaukee for Taliesin:

Mr. Wright was not at all disturbed by the fact that not one line had been drawn. As was normal, he asked me to bring him the topographical map of Bear Run, to his draughting table in the sloping-roofed studio at Taliesin, a rustic but wondrous room in itself . . . I stood by, on his right side, keeping his colored pencils sharpened. Every line he drew, vertically and especially horizontally, I watched with complete fascination . . . Mr. Kaufmann arrived and Mr. Wright greeted him in his wondrously warm manner. In the studio, Mr. Wright explained the sketches to his client. Mr. Kaufmann, a very intelligent but practical gentleman, merely said . . . "I thought you would place the house near the waterfall, not over it." Mr. Wright said quietly, "E. J., I want you to live with the waterfall, not just to look at it, but for it to become an integral part of your lives." And it did just that. That evening, my colleague Edgar Tafel and I stayed up very late and drew pencil perspectives looking up and looking down. Early the next morning, Mr. Wright

came into the studio, took my perspective, and finished it with his inevitable colored pencils.[18]

Edgar Tafel has recalled that Wright made the first three drawings that Sunday morning as Kaufmann drove toward Taliesin. In the first sketch he drew all the floor plans on top one another, with different colors to indicate the different floors [12]. Next came a north–south section through the house, and a south elevation—a straight-on view of the face of the house that came closest to being the front [13]. So far as Kaufmann knew, the drawings had been ready and waiting for some time. Wright talked about the house, then invited Kaufmann to lunch. Tafel and Mosher lingered behind, skipped the meal and dashed off two more elevation sketches before Wright and Kaufmann returned. Wright picked up the sketches and said: "And, E. J., here's the west elevation . . . and here's the north elevation."[19]

Although the sketches must have looked a bit rough to Kaufmann, they proved to be a remarkably complete presentation of the house as it would be built [14, 15]. Wright had conceived the house with an awe-inspiring finality. He was well into the fourth decade of his mature practice, and he was able to realize as much as his imagination could suggest. Behind the pencil in his hand stood an imagination as disciplined as it was free. "You see," he once wrote, "by way of concentrated thought, the idea is likely to spring into life all at once and be completed eventually with the unity of a living organism."[20] He sometimes spoke of Fallingwater as if it had been inevitable, and almost easy:

There in a beautiful forest was a solid, high rock ledge rising beside a waterfall, and the natural thing seemed to be to cantilever the house from that rock bank over the falling water . . . Then came (of course) Mr. Kaufmann's love for the beautiful site. He loved the site where the house was built and liked to listen to the waterfall. So that was a prime motive in the design. I think you can hear the waterfall when you look at the design. At least it is there, and he lives intimately with the thing he loves.[21]

When he first saw the waterfalls, Wright must have noticed the wooden bridge, the roadway turning along the rock cliff and the old Porter cottage higher on the hill. All argued for a house at the north side of the stream. Moreover, he had a rule about orientation: Any house not confined by the usual narrow city lot should be addressed "30–60" to the south, so that every room could be cheered by sunlight at least part of the day. A house built at the south side of the

[17]Wright, "In the Cause of Architecture: The Logic of the Plan," *Architectural Record*, 63 (Jan. 1928), p. 49.

[18]Letter of Jan. 20, 1974. Mosher further recalled his experiences with the house in conversations of May 15–17, 1974, at his home in Marbella, Spain, and in subsequent letters. He died in March 1992.

[19]As recalled by Tafel in a conversation of June 12, 1974.

[20]Wright, in the *Architectural Forum*, 94 (Jan. 1951), p. 93.

[21]Wright, in a conversation with Hugh Downs at Taliesin, © 1953 by the National Broadcasting Company.

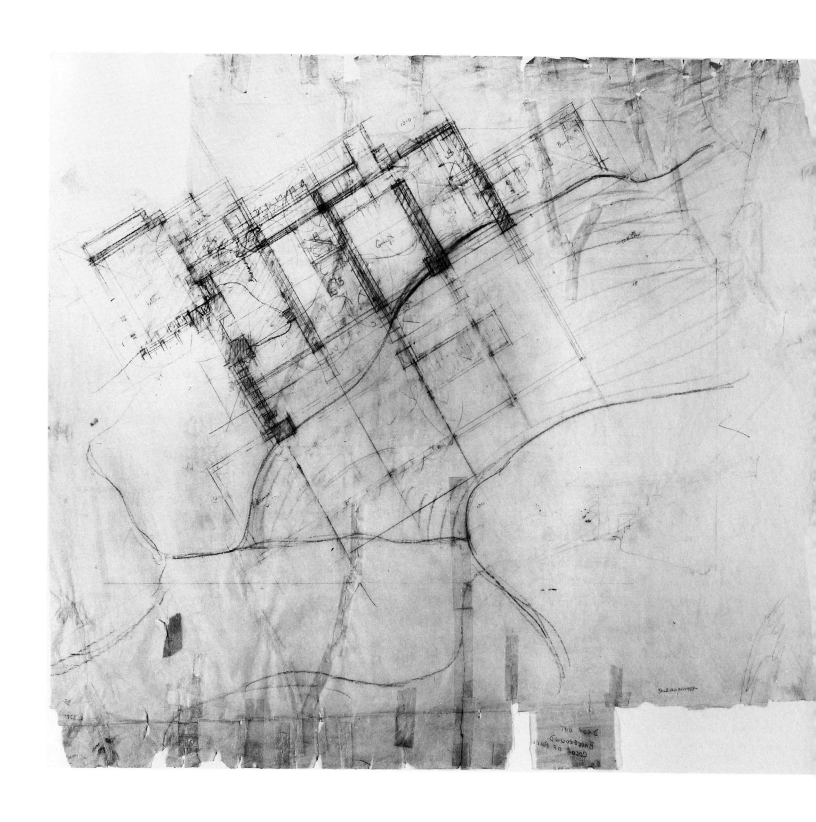

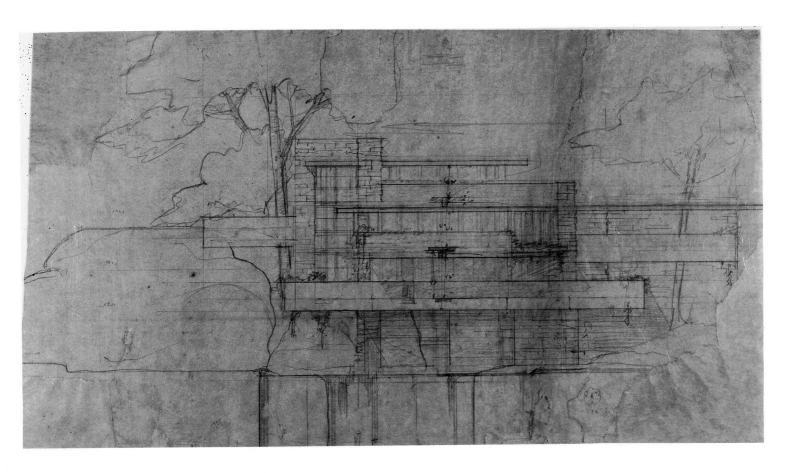

OPPOSITE: 12. First sketch of floor plans, September 1935.

ABOVE: 13. First sketch of south elevation, September 1935.

stream could be oriented to the southeast only by turning away from the most distinctive event in the forest, the falls.

To anchor the house as near as possible to the falls, between the rock outcrop and the stream, with an ideal orientation, Wright sited it parallel to the wooden bridge. He accomplished all this in his very first sketch, drawn on top the contour lines from the map. Working from the map meant that his **T** square would always establish an east–west line; by using it only to support a 30–60 triangle, with the 30-degree angle at the left and the 60-degree angle at the upper right, he would draw the south front of the house along the hypotenuse. That set the axis of orientation at 30 degrees east of due south, or seven and one-half degrees east of south-southeast. By simply turning the triangle on end he could draw every line perpendicular to the south front. All would reiterate the axis of orientation.

Any country house, by its nature, was a luxury; Kaufmann built the house on Bear Run, his son once remarked, as "a rich man's toy." The house would serve as a weekend retreat from the city and an active business life. In communion with forest and stream, it would create a place

where, in Palladio's words, "the mind, fatigued by the agitations of the city" would be "greatly restored and comforted."[22] Wright conceived the house as living space vigorously projected above the falls and into the forest, much like the ledges of rock along the cliffs and beneath the stream [16]. He had spent the long summers of his adolescent years in the Wyoming Valley of Wisconsin, where he saw thin ledges of limestone cropping out; when he came to build his home and studio there, long before he ever saw Bear Run, he had the stone walls laid up as an abstraction of the rough, random, shifting ledges.[23] Now he could imagine an entire house constituted of a series of terraces or ledges, staggered yet secure, like the ancient rock. The house would be what he called an "extension of the cliff beside a mountain stream, making living space over and above the stream upon several terraces upon which a man

[22]Andrea Palladio, *The Four Books of Architecture* (Isaac Ware edition, London, 1738; Dover reprint, 1965), Second book, chap. XII, p. 46.

[23]In talking with Hugh Downs, Wright said "the same thought applied to Taliesin that applied later to Bear Run. The site determined the features and character of Taliesin."

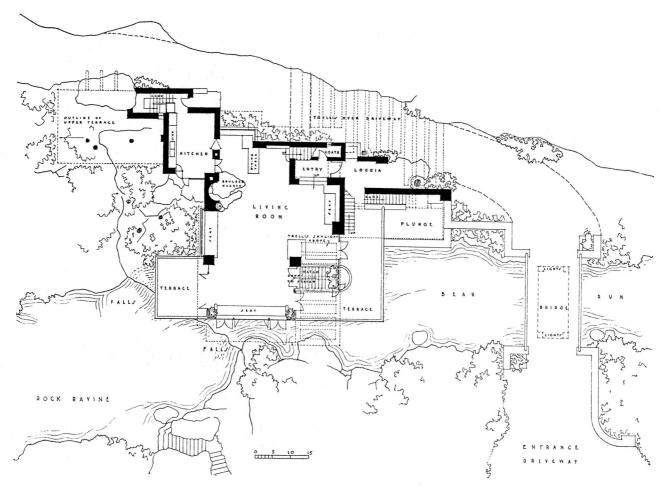

ABOVE: 14. Plan of first floor.

BELOW: 15. Plans of second and third floors, with elevations.

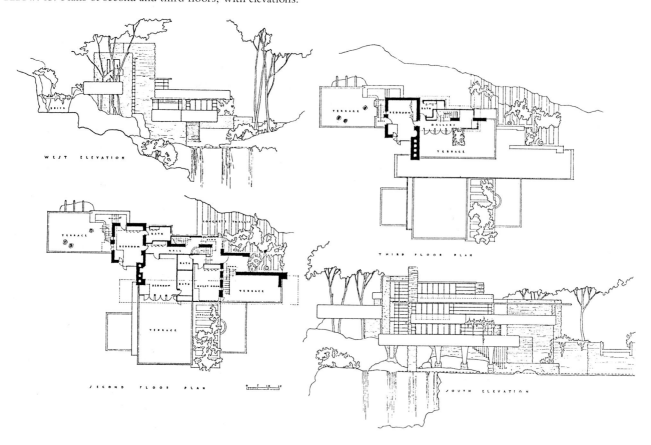

16. Rock ledges along Bear Run.

who loved the place sincerely, one who liked to listen to the waterfall, might well live."[24]

Fallingwater would complement its site but at the same time compete with the high drama of the falls, the unceasing sound of the crashing water; it would rise as a great machine in the forest [17]. Without its terraces, the whole idea of the house would vanish. But how could such terraces of living space—"leaping out," as Wright said, "from the rock ledge behind"—be constructed without intruding on the beauty of the stream? By means of the cantilever, a significant projection of structure beyond any wall or point of direct support. Cantilevers already appeared everywhere at Bear Run: not just in the rock ledges, but in the long green leaves of the laurel and rhododendron [18]. Wright

saw the cantilever as a profoundly natural principle. Engineers had used it, but with little sense of its latent poetry or expressive potential. With imagination, Wright said, the cantilever could be turned into the most romantic and free of all structural principles. It could perform remarkable feats in liberating space through swift and spirited planes parallel to the ground—the essential expression of human tenure on earth, the "true earth-line of human life, indicative of freedom."[25]

The cantilevers in the house on Bear Run would establish the horizontal with summary force: a complex, overriding rhythm of horizontal lines and planes in a precipitous and ragged place where the horizon itself could scarcely be seen [19]. A structural principle made possible that expression of architectural freedom and expansive space by which Wright meant to embody the central and unifying ideals of

[24]Wright, in the *Architectural Forum,* 68 (Jan. 1938), p. 36, Edgar Kaufmann, jr., in *Fallingwater: A Frank Lloyd Wright Country House* (New York, 1986), p. 124, asserted that the "underlying rock fault" challenged Wright by presenting "a break that called for the healing presence of architecture"; and in his 1962 reminiscence of the house wrote that Wright "healed a rift in nature." Nature, alas, hardly needs the "healing" hand of man. My perception of the house is precisely opposite: that Wright chose to echo the rift in the rock with a series of visual rifts between the successive floor levels and terraces of the house.

[25]Wright, *A Testament* (New York, 1957), p. 219, and *An Autobiography,* p. 349. Traditionally, cantilevers appear in such small-scale details as balconies and stairs, which already signify special moments of architectural space. Early in his career, Wright began to cantilever roofs to enhance an expression sympathetic to the extended horizon of the prairie landscape. His use of the cantilever grew more daring in various unexecuted projects of the 1920s.

17. Fallingwater.

18. Leaves of rhododendron.

19. Fallingwater from the southeast.

American life. The house would take a "definite masonry form" in sympathy with its site, he said, and for the first time in his experience in building residences, would call for reinforced-concrete structure. Concrete in itself was not a material he found of great interest; it lacked intrinsic character. But it was completely plastic, it could be cast into any shape and it enjoyed the great advantage of growing ever stronger with age. When reinforced with steel it gained extraordinary tensile strength. Wright had already predicted that "concrete combined with steel strands will probably become the physical body of the modern civilized world."[26]

The house would welcome changes of season, weather and light. In its darker and more secure places, shaped by the masses of stone masonry that balanced the cantilevers, it would provide a sense of refuge, in which the steady sound of the falls paradoxically reinforced the forest quiet. Wright conceived a house that far exceeded what anyone might have expected. His force of imagination spoke eloquently to what the philosopher Kant famously observed, that the spirit of genius is the very opposite of that of imitation, because its foremost property as an innate productive talent must be that of originality. "Human feeling," Wright said, "loves the vigor of spontaneity, freshness, and the charm of the unexpected."[27]

After he saw the first sketches, Kaufmann returned to

[26]Wright, "In the Cause of Architecture: Steel," *Architectural Record, 62* (Aug. 1927), p. 165.

[27]Wright, "In the Cause of Architecture: Standardization, the Soul of the Machine," *Architectural Record,* 61 (June 1927), p. 478. Also see Immanuel Kant, *Critique of Judgment* (New York, 1951), sections 46–47, pp. 150–153.

20. At work in the quarry.

Pittsburgh full of excitement. He went down to Bear Run, tried to imagine the house, and, on September 27 wrote Wright:

> I hope you will continue to work on the house plan so that we can get our preliminary sketches, floor plans and elevations at the very earliest possible time—and when they are finished that you will come to Pittsburgh with them. Let me hear from you.

Edgar Kaufmann, jr., wrote Wright the same day:

> Father spent quite some time at Bear Run showing just where the various rooms would be, and Edgar [Tafel] sent a rough drawing of the wall masses so that we are all tremendously anxious to see just what the house really will look like.
>
> As far as I am concerned, it keeps floating around in a half-formed way almost continually asking for a little more information on which to complete itself.

Preliminary plans for both the house and the office were mailed from Taliesin on October 15; Wright had left the day before, to lecture at Yale. He arrived in Pittsburgh on the 19th, for another lecture, and met Kaufmann. They visited Bear Run again, and a few days later Wright wrote that he had enjoyed his stay there immensely. Kaufmann was eager to get started by opening an old stone quarry on the hill about 500 feet west of the waterfalls; by now, he must have understood that Wright's feeling for time was quite unlike his own, and was likely to remain so. He wrote Wright on November 7 to ask what size and thickness the stones should be, and how much stone altogether would be needed. Characteristically, instead of responding, Wright waited until November 18 and then sent Kaufmann new estimates of construction costs for the house and office, from which he calculated preliminary fees of $1350. "Could you and would you send us a check for this amount," Wright wrote, "to throw into the hole at Taliesin where money ought to be and isn't?"

In a letter of November 24, Kaufmann adjusted the fees by reminding Wright that he had already sent a retainer of $250 for the house, in August. Kaufmann continued:

> Your estimate of $6,000 for the office and furniture appears rather high, although we never discussed the total amount . . .

> Your inserting the words "minimum cost of $35,000 for the house including furnishings" is a nice way of telling me that you think it is going to cost more. We sort of agreed that you were going to try to make $35,000 the maximum. However, we will work this out when the time comes.
>
> What will I do about quarrying stone this winter? Do you think it is a good idea, and if so how many perches will I need? I wrote you about this but so far have not received an answer . . .
>
> How did you solve the additional room for servants in the house? By enlarging the kitchen or giving them a separate room? Junior's and my bedrooms? Half a dozen more questions come to my mind, but as you are not in the habit of giving us progress reports while you are working on your plans, these questions remain unanswered.

After hearing nothing from Wright, he began the quarrying [20]. The masonry contractor, N. J. (Norbert James) Zeller, recalled a few months before his death in 1976 that he had his men chop lines four feet back from the edge of the rock ledge, then set off dynamite caps to break it loose. Zeller's men carried the stones down from the hill on a horse-drawn sled. "They are taking the strata of stone as it comes," Kaufmann wrote Wright on December 12, "and breaking it up into pieces about 12″ to 14″ wide and 24″ long, the thickness being the strata of the quarry. Have you any suggestions as to these sizes?"

Wright at last responded on December 16:

> Some of the stones should be as long as possible. Many of them several feet. Different lengths are desirable. So are different heights if they come out that way.
>
> The smoothest ones (not over 4″ thick) should be set aside for paving the slabs.
>
> The walls will all be a minimum of 18″ thick so some bondstones that width will be desirable.

Wright wrote another letter the same day, to thank Kaufmann for the fees paid. "We are giving you our very best," he said, "and hope it won't be just too damned good to happen."[28]

[28]Many of Wright's finest designs were unexecuted. Of one of them, the vast winter resort "San Marcos in the Desert," he wrote in *An Autobiography*, p. 315: "So, of course, it was all too good to happen. Sometimes I think it was just a dream."

Construction Begins
1936

Wright made very few changes before the first working drawings were finished in January 1936. One of them was to round the edges of the parapets and roof slabs for a more just expression of the plastic nature of the material, reinforced concrete, and to respond to the smooth curve of water over the falls. "The slabs appear rather gentler than usual," he said in 1939, "because all edges of the copings and overhangs and the slabs of the eaves are all rounded."[1] Wright also rounded in plan the parapet by the open well to the stream [21]. Once the semicircle entered his design as a lesser motif, he played it throughout the house. "The sound constitution of any entity," he wrote, "is pregnant with graceful reflexes."[2]

John H. Howe has recalled the winter of 1935–36 very well:

It would be hard to convey the excitement that we at Taliesin felt when Mr. Kaufmann asked Mr. Wright to design his house for Bear Run. This followed many years of unexecuted projects in the Taliesin studio, and together with the Johnson Wax commission indicated that the coming years would be ones of great fulfillment . . . I particularly remember Mr. Wright as he worked with relish early one morning on the perspective drawings of Fallingwater; he was dressed in his bathrobe, seated at a table by the fire in his study-bedroom. I had brought the layouts in from the studio, and was standing by with a supply of colored pencils, while he worked on the drawings. The most satisfactory and beautifully executed of these drawings was later published on the

cover of the January 17, 1938, issue of *Time* magazine, as background to Mr. Wright's portrait . . . This drawing is one which was executed entirely by Mr. Wright himself.[3]

The finest of the renderings depicted the house with all the excitement that would be captured later in photographs [22]. Bob Mosher and Edgar Tafel worked on most of the more detailed drawings; Blaine Drake has recalled that he worked on some. A few months later, when the structural calculations had to be made, Mendel Glickman and William Wesley Peters became involved [23]. Wright mailed two sets of blueprints and three sets of specifications to Pittsburgh on February 24, but Kaufmann had gone to Europe. It was April 3 before he responded:

Upon my return I found Pittsburgh in the throes of the flood condition, details of which no doubt you have heard. We are just coming through it, but in spite of it all I have had time to look at the plans and study them with no end of thrills.

We are constructing a sample wall and as soon as you return to Taliesin I think you should arrange to come to Pittsburgh as there will be a number of things to discuss.

What he did not say was that he already had sent the drawings to Morris Knowles, his consultant engineers, to be reviewed.

Abe Dombar, one of the apprentices who drove the Broadacre City models to Pittsburgh, had left the Fellowship not many months later and was working at

---

[1] Wright, *An Organic Architecture* (London, 1939), p. 38.

[2] Wright, *An Autobiography*, p. 309. Henry-Russell Hitchcock noted that "reflex" was a favorite word of Wright's, and certainly the concept was basic to his ideal of consistent character in the building as a work of art.

[3] Letter of Dec. 31, 1973. Wright was commissioned to design the Johnson Administration Building in Racine, Wis., in July 1936 and his plans were approved by the board of directors on Sept. 15, 1936; see Jonathan Lipman, *Frank Lloyd Wright and the Johnson Wax Buildings* (New York, 1986), pp. 9–39.

21. Parapet at stairwell, late 1937.

22. Rendering by Wright.

Kaufmann's Store as the assistant display architect. He and Edgar Kaufmann, jr., had been friends at Taliesin, and now they often went to Bear Run on weekends. "The plans were given to the Pittsburgh engineers," he has recalled, "to determine whether the site was capable of supporting the concentrated load of the building."[4] The engineers were not impressed by Wright's drawings or by his idea of building a house above a waterfall. They sent their report to Kaufmann on April 3:

> In accordance with your request, we have reviewed the plans prepared by Mr. Wright for your house at Bear Run, and offer the following comments . . . .
>
> 1. The end of one of the foundation walls is shown to be approximately 15 feet from the crest of the waterfall. There is a possibility of future undercutting sufficient to endanger the foundation at this point. We do not know the rate at which the falls are receding . . . .
>
> 2. At time of flood the foundation walls will deflect the main current in the stream toward the east bank at the crest of the waterfall. This may result in erosion of earth from the rock surface and tend to shift the falls to the eastward . . . [we] call your attention to the possibility of some alteration in the appearance of the falls.
>
> 3. The stone foundation walls which project into the stream—the upper one particularly—should be strong enough to withstand the battering of heavy driftwood at time of flood. We suggest that they be keyed into the rock ledge and be constructed three feet, instead of two feet, in thickness . . . .
>
> 4. We have no information concerning probable stability of the large boulder to be incorporated into the structure . . . and we question seriously the advisability of utilizing it as a part of the building foundation.
>
> 5. The plans . . . do not show dimensions of principal supporting members of the building, nor structural details such as arrangement of steel reinforcement . . . . Without this information, it is of course impossible to check the structural design of the building for strength and safety . . . .
>
> 6. . . . The plans do not show sufficient information to check the strength and stability of the proposed bridge.

[4]Letter of Apr. 4, 1975. Dombar joined the Fellowship in October 1932 and left it three years later.

23. Taliesin, late 1937. Wright with (from left) Bob Mosher, Edgar Tafel and William Wesley Peters; John Lautner, behind Wright, using a compass.

7. . . . there is always a possibility of an extreme flood, and this might bring water as high as the boiler room floor.

8. . . . approval of the state Water and Power Resources Board is required for construction or alteration of bridges, walls and other possible obstructions to stream flow . . . .[5]

Despite those expressions of educated caution, Kaufmann made haste to get started. On April 13 he wrote Wright that all the stone was quarried, sample walls had been built and a local contractor (it was Zeller, again) could make "some preliminary bids." Without the estimate Wright was to have gotten on the steel casements, Kaufmann said, the bids might be inaccurate. The next day, Wright wrote to ask $1600 for the house plans and $400 for those of the office.

Kaufmann soon would learn much about Wright that earlier clients already knew. Wright would be slow to send drawings of sufficient detail, stingy in supervision, prone to make minor changes, loath to accept blame for mistakes, slippery in promising solutions, quick to take offense and even quicker to give it. He also would be shameless in pressing for additional fees, whether or not any were due, and in soliciting outright gifts of cash. But in defending the integrity of his imagination, of what he called "the honor of the work," Wright would attain magnificent stature. The building as a work of art, conceived in rebellion against disorder and all that was mediocre, meant everything.

Wright answered Kaufmann in a second note, also dated April 14:

> I don't have much confidence in any of the usual estimates you can get on this work. We will have to plan some way of taking it up more directly with some interested competent builder who is small enough to stay on the job and experienced enough to know what to do and how to do it with our help. The steel window estimate we have is at least a thousand dollars high . . .
>
> I have a man here who can take your office work and complete it to the queen's taste.

Kaufmann responded on April 16:

> Your letter is fine but when are you coming out? Everything seems to be pivoted around your anatomy so we cannot go on until you bring it here . . .
>
> P.S. I am having the foundations staked on the property this week, and other points more for my own visualization as well as Liliane's. After all, we are only trades people and cannot see things quite as clearly as others.

The engineers in fact visited Bear Run that same day. Besides asking them to stake out the foundation lines, Kaufmann wanted them to check again for erosion, and to look more closely at the boulder Wright had chosen as the

focus of the house. Their second report, dated April 18, offered no encouragement:

> Briefly, we cannot recommend the site as suitable, from a structural standpoint, for a building of importance such as that contemplated. The rate of recession of the falls may be extremely slow, but cannot be predicted with any degree of safety . . . The question of utilizing the boulder as a base for the fireplace is perhaps a detail, but we do not consider the boulder suitable for incorporation into the foundation of the building.
>
> Of course, there is the possibility, or even a probability, that future deterioration of the rock ledge will not be sufficient to endanger the foundations; but in our opinion there could be no feeling of complete safety and consequently we recommend that the proposed site be not used for any important structure.

The report may not have reached Kaufmann before he next met Wright, who was on his way to lecture in Philadelphia and stopped off in Pittsburgh on April 19. Kaufmann and Abe Dombar met him at the railroad station, and they went down to Bear Run. Dombar wrote Wright on April 29:

> When you were here you said that I was to supervise the building of the Bear Run house, and that you would write me. No mention was made of who was to pay me or how much I was to receive—Before I ask for a leave of absence from my position at Kaufmann's, I should like to know these things—don't you think so—Please write and let me know what your wishes are—
>
> The mason has the old piers down and is starting the new masonry work tomorrow—so let's all drink a toast to the new house.

An engineer from Morris Knowles had arrived on April 28 to stake out the new bridge; he followed the center line and abutment lines of the bridge Zeller had demolished. The stream was low enough for him to poke around the upper waterfall, as he wrote in an office memorandum of May 6:

> There is a ledge of hard sand stone approximately 5 feet thick at the crest of the falls; beneath it a stratum of soft shale 1 to 2 feet thick; and below the shale more sand stone. Below the top 5-foot ledge, the falls have under-cut a distance of approximately 10 feet, or about to the location of the end of one of the foundation walls of the proposed building.

Zeller had not been working entirely on his own, because Kaufmann assigned Carl F. Thumm, the assistant manager of the store and warehouse buildings, to oversee the building activity at Bear Run and to expedite the supply of materials to the site. Thumm had experience with suppliers and tradesmen. But he was not used to Wright or to the drawings that issued from Taliesin, which seemed so deficient in details. In turn, Wright thought little of Thumm and did not want to hear from him, as he wrote Kaufmann on May 4:

[5]Copies of this report and others in the long succession of engineers' inspections of the house are in the Kaufmann collection at the Avery Library of Columbia University, New York.

You seem to forget all I said about building an extraordinary house in extraordinary circumstances. Having been through it scores of times, I know what we are up against and decline to start in unless I can see our way. The same to you.

Now suppose I were a sculptor and you would say "carve me an extraordinary statue."

I would accept.

Then you would hand me a pantagraph [sic] and say—"use this. I have found the use of the pantagraph a good way to carve statues. It saves time and money."

Then I would say—"but in this case it will waste both time and money and ruin the statue."

You would come back with "but when I have statues made I have the pantagraph used."

Well, E. J., you would have the sculptor where you have me now with your Thumb. I can't build this extraordinary house with a Thumb. Read the enclosed correspondence and note the pantagraph punctilio for only one thing. There is no sense whatever of the things he should know after studying the plans . . . .

Your Thumb won't do. I must have my own fingers. I want to make a success of this house if I have a chance. A chance means very largely having my own way with my own work using my own fingers.

Your Thumb might be helpful in his place. His place wouldn't be trying to use me (fools rush in where angels fear to tread) to get your house built, but letting me use him.

This ought to clear up point one and get me a modest builder with brains—not too anxious to show off—willing to learn new ways of doing old things. Able but wise to the fact that his previous experience might fool him in this case . . . .

Now about money.

You seem suspicious when I ask for it, and use the scissors to clip the sum. Don't be afraid. You aren't going to pay too much nor pay much too soon. You won't be let down, so don't you let me down.

When he called Taliesin to make peace, Kaufmann learned that Wright already was planning to replace Dombar. He wrote Wright on May 6:

You stated there were some additional detail plans to come through. I hope you will work on these and bring them to a conclusion immediately so that you will be in a position to send the young man you have in mind . . . .

I am very anxious to build this house for the family but I do not want to go ahead unless I know that I can complete it to your satisfaction, as the architect, as well as ours. If we build and furnish not to exceed $35,000 you must realize that we should be in a position to tell the contractor exactly what we want.

The new bridge plan has not as yet arrived and each day the contractor is working erecting the piers . . . .

Wright must have grasped the absurdity of Zeller continuing to work on the bridge without the plans; he wrote on May 8 that he was sending along the drawings. Five days later, he wrote Walter J. Hall, a builder in Port Allegany, a small town in north central Pennsylvania:

We have a house, chiefly masonry—stone work and concrete—which we are to build at Bear Run, Pennsylvania, for Mr. Edgar J. Kaufmann of Kaufmann's Department Stores in Pittsburgh. We have learned about you through one of the young men in the Taliesin Fellowship, Earl Friar, and conceived the idea that you might be of help in the construction of the house . . . .

Friar had joined the Fellowship in May 1935 to take care of the Taliesin cows. As a maintenance worker rather than an architectural apprentice, he was exempted from the annual tuition, $1100. Born and raised on a farm southwest of Gibsonburg, Ohio, he described himself as "a good milker." He first visited Taliesin in November 1934. "Taliesin is the very thing I have been groping for," he wrote Wright a few months later. Friar is remembered for having angered the master by herding cows below the sleeping quarters, early in the morning, and cursing them loudly. No one can recall what had taken him to Port Allegany, a most obscure place. Walter Hall's wife had died in 1934, and he was investing all his savings in an inn that he was building into the hillside just west of town. He called it "Lynn Hall," and it was a most romantic and Wrightian place, with a grand view over the valley. Its chances for success were much reduced, however, by the firm stance Hall took against serving alcohol. Oddly enough, Wright's son John Lloyd Wright, an architect himself, also had encountered Hall and his roadside dream. Hall was born in Port Allegany in 1878 and had become a builder before the turn of the century. He had watched Wright at work on the Larkin Building in Buffalo, New York, around 1905, and had admired him ever since. He answered Wright's letter on May 23:

During a period of nearly forty years of active building experience (I am now 57), it has been my lot to build many small and medium sized houses; most of which should have been remodeled the day they were finished—due in part at least to my inability to make untractable clients see the truth in matters of design. After all these years it certainly would be a pleasure to work on a house where this obstacle to success would be removed . . . .

Incidentally, I have never worked on a job over which I did not have complete charge. In this connection it may be well to mention that my experience with the labor unions has been similar to your own at Midway Gardens. This might possibly be a stumbling block in [the] way of my employment on this house.

Since contracting has proven unprofitable for the past several years, I have ventured building an inn for myself on a new section of the Roosevelt Highway [U.S. Route 6]. For this structure, in which your son John seemed very interested, I

24. Walter J. Hall with his "boys."

took the sand and stone from the hill at the site and carried on the work almost entirely with my own hands . . . .[6]

Hall clearly was a man of Wright's stripe, and his letter was well received [24]. "From what I can learn of this man," Wright wrote Kaufmann, "he would be the one to build your house for us. Won't you look him up in your way so when we come down to meet him there will be no kick-backs?"

Dombar, meantime, was upset by not being paid for his service as clerk-of-the-works:

I told Mr. K. that I hadn't been receiving any salary. According to the architect-owner agreement he had been sending supervision money to Taliesin; it was up to them to pay me; I phoned Mr. W., who indicated that to him I still was an

[6]John Lloyd Wright (1892–1972), the architect's second son, worked for his father in making drawings for the Midway Gardens of 1913–14 in Chicago, and in supervising its construction. See his memoir, *My Father Who Is on Earth* (New York, 1946; Dover reprint, 1992). From a document filed at the time of Hall's death in 1952 it appears that he was in fact 58 when he first wrote Wright.

25. Bridge, October 1936.

"apprentice" and should not have expected to be paid. The Kaufmanns took care of my meals . . . so I tried to accept Mr. Wright's attitude on the matter. Soon the apprentices at Taliesin were complaining that the "rebel," who had left the Fellowship, was being rewarded with the juicy plum, and so the following month Mr. W. brought out Bob Mosher to take over my duties.

The revised working drawings were finished May 27, and a few days later Wright headed East with Mosher, Edgar Tafel and Manuel Sandoval. The man Wright said would build Kaufmann's office "to the queen's taste" was Sandoval, an apprentice from Nicaragua. "He had come to Taliesin, he thought, to study architecture," Tafel has recalled. "Once his real talents were known, however, Mr. Wright never let him out of the woodworking shop. Manuel's reverence for Mr. Wright was such that he made an elegant velvet-lined box to store a pencil given to him by Mr. Wright."[7]

[7]*Years With Frank Lloyd Wright*, p. 85.

On the way to Pittsburgh, they deviated to Buffalo to see the Larkin Building and the Darwin D. Martin house: his buildings, said Wright, were as if his children. They arrived in Pittsburgh on Friday, June 5, and a contract was signed for the office interior. It specified that the office was to be finished by September 15; Kaufmann had no reason to suspect that Wright would allow the project to drag on for a year and a half.

Everyone went down to Bear Run that weekend, and found Zeller making a poor job of the new bridge. Some of the stonework lacked the vital character Wright was after, and the concrete parapets looked indecisive, even limp [25]. Much later, the bridge would be rebuilt to new drawings, and the stonework would gain a syncopated rhythm of random ledges, or "stickouts": a rough and yet sophisticated abstraction of the native sedimentary beds [26, 27]. Byron Keeler Mosher, the apprentice Wright picked to replace Dombar, was a short and alert young man who worried about his name. He had yellow hair and a quick, broad smile, which led Wright to call him "Little Sunshine," a

26. Bridge rebuilt.

27. Rhythm in stonework of bridge abutment.

name he later recalled without evident joy. He did not even like his given name, Byron, and was so intent on being called Bob that he took his diploma from the University of Michigan as Robert Keeler Mosher. He always thought Wright was fond of him because he asked questions of the sort that the more fawning apprentices were scared to ask. Mosher found himself worried at Bear Run not so much by the misshapen bridge as by the lay of the land. How, in that wild place, could he find the "datum," the elevation of the first floor? The plot plan took note of four boulders on the north side of the stream. One would be under the living-room floor, virtually a fulcrum on which the house would balance—as one of the most beautiful drawings, a section looking west, made clear [28]. It was Wright's understanding that this boulder was Kaufmann's favorite place for lying in the sun and listening to the falls. He told some of the apprentices he was going to put it at the heart of the house, in fact make it the hearth.

Mosher asked about the datum, and Wright told him to get through the rhododendrons and on top the boulder; then he should know. Up on the boulder, Mosher was not standing much higher than Wright, who was down by the bridge: The roadway across the bridge was built at 1309.5 feet above sea level, and the datum of the boulder was 1311.7 feet. Wright's attention to the site was so keen that the act of crossing the bridge, a span of more than 28 feet, and approaching the main entrance of the house, about 60

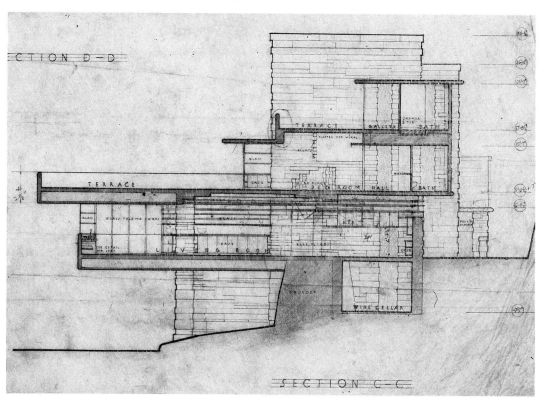

28. Section looking west.

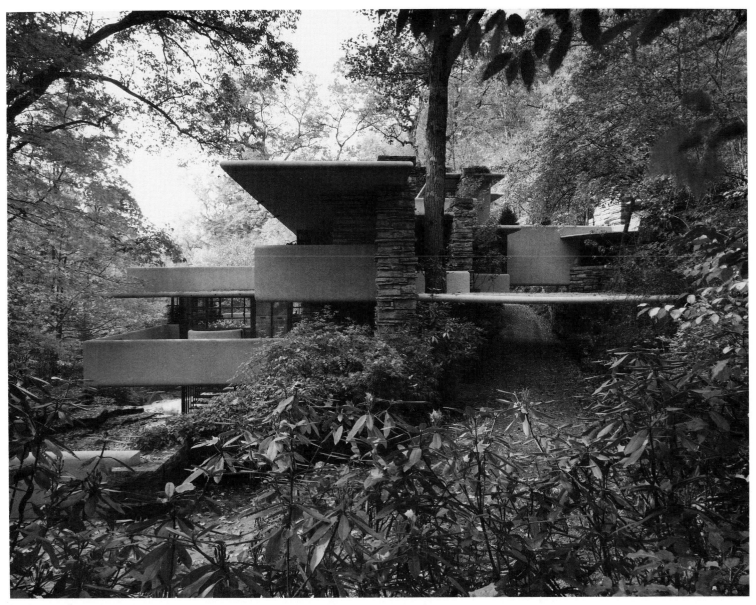

29. Approach to entrance.

feet past the bridge, would always seem an uphill journey into a private territory, even though the entrance, at three steps below the living-room floor, was only six inches higher than the bridge roadway [29]. And such was Wright's mastery of horizontal rhythms in line and plane, that although the chimney mass would rise more than 30 feet above the living-room floor, the house from every point would look very low to the ground [30].

After the other apprentices and Wright left Bear Run that Saturday evening, June 6, Mosher reviewed the working drawings with Kaufmann until 1 o'clock in the morning. They studied the drawings again on Sunday, and Thumm arrived. "It seemed as if I had met him before," Mosher

soon wrote Wright. "He wants to be called upon for advice *when* that advice is needed."

The engineers from Pittsburgh had not taken much care in staking out the house; Mosher discovered a three-inch leeway in the 36 feet that represented three of the units Wright used to establish a regular system of bays, or what John Lautner has recalled as the "horizontal module to suit the rock foundations in the stream." The plan of the house could fit almost perfectly within a 60-foot square, five horizontal units in each direction. The west bay defined the kitchen and two bedrooms above. Next came two bays that formed the central space of the living room and accounted for Mrs. Kaufmann's room, directly above, and

30. Horizontal planes, late 1937.

the long gallery at the third story. The fourth bay subsumed the hatch to the stream, the skylighted reading area and the music alcove; and the last bay encompassed the east living-room terrace and the entrance loggia.

Vertical dimensions were to be controlled by a second unit, only 17 inches. Both unit systems, as Wright called them, were meant to sustain proportions—not to generate predictable or routine symmetries. The west living-room terrace, or balcony, would extend about two feet beyond the horizontal unit-line to magnify the drama of the cantilever and to avert any obvious display of the bay; and the central space of the living room, as a doubled unit of 24 feet, would not express one of the major piers below it.

Nor could the inherent discipline of the bays greatly reduce the complexity of the building-project. Mosher also was faced by rainy weather, untutored workmen and his own lack of experience. He nevertheless found his responsibilities exhilarating. Bear Run took on "the kind of chaos the builder revels in," he wrote Wright on June 11:

Tuesday [June 9] the great tree came crashing down and the sunlight poured in to dry things up considerably. We took it down in three pieces and the engineering required to land it in the only space possible without harm was interesting. Seven men and a team seemed superfluous, but all were used. Next, all the hampering brush; then it was surprising to see the sense of increased space. From the bridge the site looks tremendous and consequently quite thrilling . . . .

Having a fairly good time with the workmen, especially the stonemasons. They seem to be a reasonably good crowd, all young, not like the Wisconsin riff-raff. But they need watching every minute. A number of times I have caught them doing peculiar things to rocks such as setting them on end . . . Yesterday I made them tear a pier down that I didn't like. It had gotten up about three feet and just wasn't good. I've got them to the point now where they'll stand back and look at it and then yell for me if not sure . . . .

The hapless Zeller lasted only a week after Wright left Bear Run. Mosher related the circumstances in a letter of June 16:

A little difficulty arose last Saturday [June 13] when the stonemason foreman, Zeller, was put into jail for non-support. The Squire, as such officials are called here, phoned Mr. Kaufmann to go the $500 bond. The bond refused, I am now filling the capacity of the man behind the bars . . . I now have complete charge of a dozen men, I hire them and fire them as well, I order and bill all materials, take care of their time, wages, and payroll. Zeller's contract being broken, he will not be back; he was of little use . . . .

I have become fairly well enough acquainted with the vicinity so that I can increase help when necessary. Many of them are the typical country laborers, slow and irresponsible, and so I have had to change from time to time. Stonemasons are scarce; the ever-present WPA continues to have and to hold . . . .

Only a few months before his death in 1976, Zeller could

recall that his wife was told that weekend about nude sunbathing at Bear Run. After she brought the charges, Zeller said, she told Kaufmann her husband would not be returning to build any nudist colony. "Bare Run" persists even today as a local play on words.

Mosher now worked four weeks without a contractor. He saw the retaining walls rise between the bridge and where the house was to be, he began other walls and he confronted the boulders—which turned out to be larger, more frequent and located otherwise than shown on the plot plan. He was sending many more reports and queries than Wright cared to answer, and that made his position even more difficult. He continued to worry about the character of the stonework. "I have still to watch the stonemasons carefully," he wrote on June 18, "and occasionally a rock gets in that looks a bit bull-eyeish." But he stayed in high spirits:

each day's work is making Bear Run more and more exciting, so that the end of each day brings on hopes for twice as much accomplished tomorrow . . . I become very impatient when I see how thrilling the structure will be, so much more so than any drawing could present it. The beauty of the site, in spite of being in the valley, is contagious.

One characteristic detail of the house, designed after construction got under way, was broached by Mosher on June 16 and again when he wrote Wright on June 25:

Enclosed is a rough sketch (my drawing equipment extremely limited) of a scheme of mine for overcoming the difficulty of the stone stairs which would otherwise end about four feet up in the air because the bank which we indicated on our plans is non-existent. The Kaufmanns seem to want a plunge somewhat of the type which they now have in the small cottage. So if we let the steps come right down into the water of a terraced pool it would not be necessary to increase the length of the present pier that supports the stairs. The pool would be about four feet deep or more . . . The low retaining wall could be the same height as the stone piers of the bolsters. I think the result would tie in fairly well, with the water overflowing continuously into the stream and one end devoted to plants and fernery.

The stairs or outside pier of the stairs have not been started. I shall wait for your suggestions.

Earlier that month, Wright injured himself trying to run a road grader. Despite his 69 years, he quickly recovered. The lack of an experienced builder at Bear Run gave him time to reconsider the structural system. His sense of structure was largely intuitive, just like his feeling for nature—which, indeed, often inspired his structural ideas. The danger, of course, arose when his ideas outdistanced the means at hand, or entered realms where the "slide-rule engineers," as he called them, would not go.[8] Because his own training as an engineer had been so slight, he relied on Peters and Glickman.

[8]Wright, *An Autobiography,* pp. 343, 479.

William Wesley Peters had joined the Fellowship at its beginning, when he was only 20 years old and fresh from two years at the Massachusetts Institute of Technology. He was loyal, handsome, strong and so tall that he could not walk through Wright's house entirely at ease, especially when Wright would say, "Wes, sit down—you're ruining the scale of my architecture!" Peters was one of Wright's favorite apprentices. One spring morning in 1935 he drove off with a young woman named Svetlana, who was Mrs. Wright's daughter by an earlier marriage. Wright and his wife thought she was too young to be getting married, so Peters and his bride were estranged from the Fellowship for about a year. Peters missed the early drawings for Fallingwater. But after he returned to Taliesin he stayed there until his death in July 1991.

Mendel Glickman was not an apprentice; he was older, and he was already an accomplished architectural engineer. Mosher recalled that when he first arrived at Taliesin, on October 24, 1932, it was Glickman who took him in to meet Wright. Glickman and his wife were there several months before the Fellowship got under way; in 1931 they had returned from Russia, where Glickman, who was born in Vitebsk in 1895, served as the chief American engineer for the construction and production-line development of the first tractor factory in what for a time was called Stalingrad. Glickman did not stay long at Taliesin—married couples rarely found the communal pattern of life very satisfactory—but he remained dedicated to Wright all his life, and always on call as a consultant engineer. He spent a few days at Taliesin at the end of June 1936, and he was summoned there again on July 9 to work out the structural changes Wright wanted in the cantilever slabs.

What claimed Mosher's attention toward the end of June were the stone piers and concrete "bolsters" that would rise as though on tiptoe to help support the cantilever of the first floor. Wright ignored the Pittsburgh engineers when they recommended that the stone footings be widened to three feet, rather than two, to better resist battering during floods. He was intent instead on the look of the bolsters. In his earliest sketches, he stepped them out something like a short flight of stairs, to generate long horizontal shadow lines.[9] The motif had style, but was not entirely valid for vertical supports in reinforced concrete. Wright had spoken in 1930 at Princeton University about the utmost importance of plasticity, in which "the quality and nature of materials are seen 'flowing or growing' into form instead of

seen as built up out of cut and joined pieces."[10] Now he redesigned the bolsters to flare continuously from 15 inches wide at their bases to more than three feet wide at the floor slab, which they were to meet with graceful curves struck from a seven-inch radius. No one forewarned Mosher. The new drawing, dated July 1, arrived too late. "The bolsters have been stripped and floated," he wrote on July 4. "They look their part, which means they are exciting even more than expected." Mosher not only got a new drawing; he was chastised for having devised long slots in the stone piers to accept the concrete bolsters. "This horizontal groove was not indicated anywhere in the drawings," Tafel wrote, "and Mr. Wright says: 'Don't start improvising.' "

When he sited the house above the falls and on top the boulders, Wright radically changed forever Kaufmann's favorite place in the forest. He also threatened the family's habits of weekend relaxation. Kaufmann particularly wanted some way to swim, but Wright continued to resist his ideas for an artificial pool so close by a natural course of water. Mosher wrote on July 4:

As the work progresses the Kaufmanns are becoming all the more enthused and spend a good deal of time here in order to see the work . . . E. J. pours over everything with a good deal of precision . . . .

This is Mr. Kaufmann's sentiment about the function that water will play in relation to the house: That over half of the time in the summer months that are spent here swimming, bathing, and sunning are rigidly adhered to, and that their functions are indispensable to the life of the house . . . .

Of the two desired solutions to the water problem the first is the absolute necessity, that is, a small plunge placed at the foot of the small stairs or elsewhere convenient to access; and second, and by far the preferred, the pool for swimming and a place or platform for sunning.

Wright eventually accepted Mosher's suggestions for tucking a small plunge into the cluster of stone walls at the east end of the house. The drawing was dated August 20, but the plunge was not built until 1937 [31]. In summer months, when the plunge was full, it was about five feet deep, and it spilled gently over the low stone wall into the stream.

Wright grew impatient over the absence of a trained builder at Bear Run. He found Mosher's frequent queries bothersome, and he got angry when letters arrived from Kaufmann's aides. Tafel expressed all those feelings when he wrote Mosher on July 9:

Mr. Wright will ignore letters from the Thumms and Silvermans . . . You get the bids on all business and you ask for drawings. Nobody else. If this other comes in (Thumms and Silvermans) the whole system will go to pot . . .

---

[9]This form of streamlining in horizontal overlaps, stepped out and up, dated back at least to 1922 in Wright's work. His eldest son, Lloyd Wright, in a letter of Jan. 23, 1976, wrote that traditional American clapboarding, "while practical as sheathing, was in the view of my father and myself aesthetically weak and cheap and characterless. So when we were making studies for the Tahoe cabins we indicated a bolder detail . . . overlaps of the siding holding the siding face not pitched—as on the typical milled lapped siding—but vertical, and with the thickness of the wood siding gaining richness and strength structurally as well as visually . . . ."

[10]Wright, *Modern Architecture* (Princeton, N.J., 1931), p. 30. In *An Autobiography*, p. 341, he wrote of the supported growing from the support "somewhat as a tree-branch glides out of its tree trunk."

Mr. Wright wants you to stop fussing with those boulders [in the basement] and let them come as they are: no plaster or anything on them. Just as the plans read.

We trust you are not going above the kitchen floor level with the stonework until you have Mr. Wright's drawing for the slab construction . . . .

Mr. Wright says you are being used too much in capacity of a workman rather than a superintendent. Let us know what you will do about it.

Mosher must have been stung; it was a week before he answered:

I don't think I have been used to disadvantage, at least not to myself. Certainly the work that has kept me so confined has been that of superintending and not that of laboring. But superintending has meant running the gamut from A to Z . . . .

The means of communication are against us, I know. It takes so long to hear . . . Mr. Kaufmann has kept me close to him, talking, asking questions, a great deal of the time he spends here. He knows every inch of the plans . . . .

I will say that of the contact that I have had to have with Mr. Thumm he has been most congenial and helpful. But I realize the circumstances and shall try to eliminate any pressure from that source.

And now Mr. Hall. I am very glad he is here and I have every ounce of confidence in his ability. He reveres you and has been yours ever since that day he saw you (but afraid to approach you then) on the grounds during the construction of the Larkin Building. He has given up his own work to come here and he feels now very happy that he did . . . .

Mr. Hall states that he will continue with the forms but does not wish to go ahead with the steel ordering and work until he receives the structural details from you.

Despite the inaccuracies of the plot plan and all his encounters with the boulders, Mosher had carelessly injured himself:

I've had a slight mishap too. One of these very hot nights after one of these very hot days about ten o'clock when I was falling fast asleep at my desk and had plenty more work to do, I decided to revive myself with a swim. And in the dark I dove off a high rock, hit bottom or something and the next day and for three days after was unable to move my neck. My center of gravity just shifted over six inches. Now it's all much better . . . I shall use the springboard hereafter in the dark.

"How could he do that?" Wright asked. "Bob looked at the plot plan," Tafel answered, "saw where it said water, and dove in." The master was not amused.

Wright had warned Kaufmann on July 10 that he was not going to send the structural details until a competent builder arrived. "If Hall has fallen down," Wright telegraphed, "must seek someone else." He also telegraphed

31. Steps to plunge. Bronze sculpture is *Mother and Child* by Jacques Lipchitz, 1941–45.

Hall: "Kaufmann evidently worn out by lack of prompt cooperation on your part. Must have someone at once to go on with construction." Hall had met with Kaufmann and come to terms, but he was waiting for a written contract; Thumm had remarked that other candidates asked less money. The mere mention of Thumm set off Wright again. He wrote Kaufmann on July 13:

A note from Hall says he is on the job now and would have been ten days ago but for your Thumm in the soup again.

These officious yes-men make their boss more trouble in the end than they could ever pay for in cheese-parings. Isn't that style of business distinctly dated? I thought so.

Hall reached Bear Run the night of July 13. Earlier in the day, he and Kaufmann signed a five-page contract. It had but few salient points:

Each week Mr. Kaufmann will pay the sum of $50 to Mr. Hall as wages for services rendered . . . .

Previous to entering into this agreement, Mr. Hall carefully examined the plans and specifications and prepared an esti-

ABOVE: 32. Narrow stairs to plunge.
BELOW: 33. Stone basin by entrance.

mate covering the cost of the building. The total amount of this estimate is $29,000. Now, if Mr. Hall does complete the entire work, in accordance with the plans and specifications for a total cost not to exceed his beforementioned estimate, then Mr. Kaufmann agrees to further reimburse Mr. Hall with a cash bonus equal to $25 per week for each and every week Mr. Hall remains in the employ of Mr. Kaufmann on this work.

After the middle of July, Wright became preoccupied with a commission of great importance, the Johnson Wax Building in Racine, Wisconsin. Mosher had continued to pepper him with questions and suggestions, and Wright took even longer to answer. The kitchen would be better ventilated, Mosher thought, if he could add a tall casement near the door to the drive; Wright said no. Mrs. Kaufmann wanted to reverse the sequence of the two basement rooms, Mosher wrote, so the combination wine room and fruit cellar would be next to the kitchen stairs and the boiler room farther to the east. Wright agreed. "Mr. Kaufmann says he has a feeling he is going to get fatter as he gets older," Mosher wrote on July 16, asking permission to widen the stairs toward the plunge from 30 inches to three or three and a half feet. Wright refused; but the stone steps—originally planned as concrete steps—were built about 34 inches wide [32]. Mosher wrote on July 26 about a basin proposed at the main entry:

> And then the Entry took another hour, and more suggestions. And the introduction of a feature when Mr. Kaufmann and Junior got their heads together (everything was fine before he appeared on the scene). And that is instead of the wardrobe at the end of the entry, a tricky water receptacle for the purpose of rinsing hands taking place of lavatory, of taking care of flowers (vase filling and that sort of thing) and an overflow below to clean feet in, from bathing. Sounds to me like a baptismal font, and that crossing oneself would be in order . . . I suggested instead of Junie's basin idea a low little pool . . . water could drop into it from the wall . . . .

Wright responded that "slopping about" at the entry did not appeal to him, but three weeks later he accepted Mosher's notion and recommended a simple stone bath outside the entry "where flowers can be thrown in it to keep them fresh and our clients can dip their feet without wetting the entry floor." And that was what was built [33].

Kaufmann wanted his bed closer to the south bay of windows, and he thought the west bedroom terrace might well be lowered to the same elevation as the second floor. Wright wrote Mosher on July 29:

> I do not want to drop the terrace floor now affixed to the boulder. I like very much its natural relation to the two upper stories. It does the house harm to "level up" this terrace . . . .
>
> Senior Kaufmann's room can be as he wants it.

Hall had poured the new bolsters on July 22, and he stripped the forms early in August [34, 35]. Mosher appre-

ABOVE: 34. Bolsters and stairwell, October 1936.

BELOW: 35. Finished bolsters and stairs to stream. (Ezra Stoller © ESTO.)

ciated the change. "They are great heavy masses, to be sure," he wrote Wright, "but slender enough to be extremely graceful. I like them so much more than the original." Later that month, Mosher expressed concern that the stairs planned from the living-room hatch to the stream might be ruined in floods. He also offered several sketches for other steps, off the west side of the house and down to the stream below the waterfall. Wright answered on August 21 by defining the very nature of the house:

> In discussing matters with our client it is well to have in mind the motif of the building—that is to say, the reason why it is as it is where it is.

> We got down into that glen to associate directly with the stream and planned the house for that association. Hence the steps from living room to stream. I intended to deepen the stream for a swimming pool under the house at the foot of these steps. With artificial collateral pools we look foolish.

Again, the main floor is a projecting *balcony* over the stream. To put stairs from the balcony to the ground robs the balcony of any character or romance as such.

> The stonework was intended to blend with that of the glen. But the walls built before we got there do not . . . .

> In view of our building as in the glen to associate with and play with the natural stream, it might be all right to dam the stream itself in some natural way in keeping with the rocks that are its boundary. Say, just above the falls to make a ripple or two before the deep fall and so make the stream itself deep enough for a plunge under the house . . . some blasting could be done by someone who knows how . . . I should think five feet ample for depth of water, or perhaps four.

Weeks had passed while the formwork was being readied for the cantilever slab of the first floor. Every other aspect of the house paled by comparison to the great cantilever; the floor slab was to project 18 feet past the stone piers be-

neath the bolsters [36]. Kaufmann was worried. He turned for reassurance to the Metzger-Richardson Company, a Pittsburgh firm of registered engineers and suppliers of steel for concrete. Metzger-Richardson made new drawings for the slab reinforcement; finished on August 10, they were not based on Wright's specifications. "At the time we furnished the steel for these beams," the engineers wrote later, "we put in twice as much steel as was called for on the plans."[11]

The new order of steel reached Bear Run on August 15, and everything was in place by August 19. "Hall pouring today," Mosher telegraphed Wright two days later. "Wire change immediately, if any. Difficulty to hold him back once started." A few days later, Hall wrote Wright:

> After many delays the first floor slab is poured and today I moved the upper forms and I am quite happy over the result. Everything lines up straighter than a schoolmarm's leg.
>
> Building in the creek with posts under water is always uncertain as to bearing, which could easily make a crack in the parapet. The result has relieved me of a lot of worry.
>
> The way the stone work is laid is causing me a lot of worry as to whether or not it will please you. We are just starting the living-room stone work tomorrow . . . . The quarry since you were here has run larger stones. As it stands, I fear we are practicing on Mr. Kaufmann so that we can build a better stone job the next time.
>
> Another thing that has caused me a lot of annoyance is that Bob [Mosher] is the only one that doesn't get any money out of this work. You, Mr. Kaufmann and myself riding him without money is not right . . . .

Two mistakes were made when the first-floor cantilever was poured. One enraged Wright, the other resulted in the drooping lines that haunted Kaufmann for the rest of his life. First, a dozen steel bars were inserted "surreptitiously" as Mosher put it. Second, no one paid attention to the inescapable force of gravity: the slab was poured at true level instead of being canted slightly to compensate for later deflection. Hall thought a well-poured cantilever slab would *rise* a little as the concrete cured, letting the formwork fall free. The surreptitious steel bars, each one inch square, were placed in the four major floor beams. Each beam was two feet wide, and the concrete joists or "ribs" between the beams were about four inches thick and spaced four feet apart. Hall had suggested hollow tile, but Wright said the concrete ribs would be a working part "of the structural integrity of the whole fabric." To accommodate the hatch to the stream, the most eastward beam followed a semicircular detour. It swelled to three feet wide to support a subsidiary cantilever, that of the east living-room terrace [37].

37. Curved floor-beam, October 1936.

The hatch and hanging steps seemed to Kaufmann a willful complication and one without purpose. He still was intent on swimming, and without telling Wright he asked Metzger-Richardson how the west bedroom terrace might be changed into a diving pool. Thumm duly recorded on August 26 that he had given Mosher a tracing of "our engineering idea as to the swimming pool" by Kaufmann's bedroom, and expected him to "develop the architectural features of the pool . . . so that we may have the engineer develop same structurally."

Wright heard nothing about Metzger-Richardson's role, or their doubled order of steel for the first-floor slab, until he received a letter of Mosher's dated August 25:

> The slab is poured. The long waited-for epoch has now opened new fields . . . .
>
> But now I feel that your presence is needed . . . .
>
> First, Hall, as a figure in the picture, has need to become better equipped in our necessary procedure of building, which seems to irritate him considerably now. He is being trained but not fast enough for the benefit of the building . . . .
>
> Secondly, the stonework so far should be studied before progressing into the upper floors and interiors. I have to argue for larger stones all through the game, and even now I don't feel that the scale is just what it ought to be . . . The stonework has been an arguing point all the way through . . . You can settle this on sight.
>
> Thirdly, the concrete work is well along now and its procedure to me has seemed a bit too haphazard. I may be wrong, however. But the slab has been poured to three different times, and when the forms to the parapets [were] stripped,

[11]Report of June 1, 1937, by the Metzger-Richardson Co. to Edgar J. Kaufmann, p. 4.

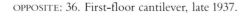

OPPOSITE: 36. First-floor cantilever, late 1937.

there have been holes and cavities showing so that the whole thing immediately was gone over with a rich mix and then floated with a white cement . . . using fine white sand. I questioned this severely, but Hall insisted he knew what he was doing. I argued for about two hours Sunday [August 23] with the client and Hall about finish. They wanted a glass-smooth surface, no sand, no texture; to me it was horrible, Internationalish, and sterile and hard . . . Hall is insistent on his own likes and dislikes and displays them to Kaufmann, and I have to step down on both of them . . . Pet comeback from client: "I'm the one who's living in this house, not the architect, and I want it this way." Then I do argue more than ever. "What does the architect know what I want," says he, and so on and so on . . . .

I am enclosing some calculations made in Pittsburgh by engineers hired by Kaufmann: their contention was that more steel [was] necessary in beams because they discovered that the weight of [the] second floor transposed through T-iron window frames was not figured. Steel was sent out and put in at last moment. Our builder does not trust us . . . .

Wright exploded. He wrote Kaufmann on August 27:

If you are paying to have the concrete engineering done down there, there is no use whatever in our doing it here. I am willing you should take it over but I am not willing to be insulted.

So we will send no more steel diagrams. I am unaccustomed to such treatment where I have built buildings before and do not intend to put up with it now, so I am calling Bob back until we can work out something or nothing.

Also it appears that an attitude has developed on your part— "What does the architect know about what I want—I am going to live in this house—not he." Now I have heard that provincialism from women but never before from a man. And it isn't too late yet for you to get an architect that does know what you want.

I don't know what kind of architect you are familiar with but it apparently isn't the kind I think I am. You seem not to know how to treat a decent one. I have put so much more into this house than you or any other client has a right to expect that if I haven't your confidence—to hell with the whole thing.

The same day, Wright telegraphed Mosher:

Drop work and come back immediately. We are through until Kaufmann and I arrive at some basis of mutual respect. You are needed here. Do not delay one hour and bring all plans you can get. If you have no money draw on me Farmers State Bank.

Mosher must have balked, for Wright sent another telegram:

You are at least able to get off the job as instructed. Neither explanation nor argument should be necessary. My affairs there more serious than you comprehend. If you are unable or unwilling to carry out my instructions your connection with me ends. I am not coming to Pittsburgh.

Kaufmann responded with a letter that mimicked Wright's almost line by line. He asked Wright to inspect Hall's work, and he protested that the plans did not yet indicate how the house would accommodate "certain elements in our living at Bear Run that are so much a part of our lives, such as water and outdoor sleeping." Wright meantime took aim at Hall in a letter of August 29:

Probably you have always been your own boss, never worked for an architect and never heard of ethics . . . .

If you imagine your meddlesome attitude to be either sensible or honest (we will not say ethical) something was left out of either your character or your education.

I have put too much into this house (even *money*, which item you will understand) to have it miscarry by mischievous interferences of any sort. The kind of buildings I build don't happen that way. (Several have been ruined that way, however.) And this one may be one of them.

It is only fair to say to you directly that you will either fish or cut bait or I will. I am willing to quit, if I must, but unwilling to go on with my eyes open into the failure of my work . . . .

Failure, I mean, by way of treacherous interference.

The next day he wrote Kaufmann to argue that the steel bars would weaken the structure with their excess weight. He lashed Kaufmann again:

I thought I had found a man and a client. But is this your usual method in dealing with men? If so, I will make a prophecy—In ten years time no one will work for you for either love or money.

I have worked for much of one in your case and a little of the other. So damned little of the other (money) that it hardly matters . . . And for this you hand me this betrayal to solve your own fear—If you were afraid why didn't you say so? . . .

Now maybe these pearls of wisdom gained by experience have been cast before swine and not only do the swine refuse to eat the pearls but turn and rend us.

What do you think?

Does any client really know when he is well off?

Wright finally began the process of reconciliation with an eloquent letter he wrote Kaufmann on August 31:

A man's work is his honor . . . had I thought less of you I should have been more polite, not outrageous.

At any rate Bob should come back here for a cinch in his belt. He needs a little seasoning perhaps. He'll get it. Perhaps I need it too. I'll get it . . . .

The kind of thing I laid out with you was for you and is so in every detail but *the details must be mine.* I am your technician and any interference from others will be particularly offensive because the concentration is most intense. The more so as the work becomes more difficult and specialized.

Apologies are nothing to a man like yourself. But explanation seems to be in order. The atmosphere should be cleared. Lightning and inevitable thunder may help to clear it . . . .

I am master-builder where I have conceived or I am nothing. But if you are not convinced that I am faithfully interpreting your desires where a way of life is concerned with a building—and that your way of life, as you see it, is my first and deepest concern—then I don't know how to convince you.

You can only say—"the fool doesn't know life as I know it"—and get rid of me.

It has never been difficult for anyone to get rid of me.

Kaufmann telegraphed Wright that his letter helped explain many thoughts and was "most satisfactory." He asked Wright to return to Bear Run with "someone to pick up where Bob Mosher left off." Wright seemed agreeable, but decided later to leave Hall on his own.

The unit-system Wright favored in place of fully explicit dimensions confused Hall as much as it did Thumm. Hall wrote Wright on September 12:

I had quite a time today locating the two 30 by 36 inch piers in the living room. To keep going I had to locate them by guess and by God rather than any figures I could find from the unit line. For the good of the party who made these plans I wish you would impress upon them how dumb Hall is, and to give better measurements to builders of this kind . . . .

I wish to assure you there will not be the usual contractor-owner combination setup to change architect plans; however it is Mr. Kaufmann's and my nature to antagonize anybody that can't take it, so tell the party you send out to try to hold his own with us and it will be a great training for him.

Hall was happy enough without a clerk-of-the-works, as he wrote on September 16:

Another thing has occurred to me since you left. If you are very busy with the party you were going to send down to help me, you could delay sending them at present. I have a combination cook and typist who comes in the evening, gets my dinner and stays for any correspondence. This is a great help with the work; besides, she is good looking and I would rather not have [a] third party around.

However, if you would be better satisfied and do not need the boy at home, I will ditch the girl and work the party you send down enough to pay for his board . . . Pick out a well rounded boy, one you think can carry your work on after you are gone.

His own arrangement with Kaufmann, he continued, would net him only a few hundred dollars and the satisfaction of having built a house designed by Wright. A few days later, Hall wrote that "as the work progresses, and the beauty of the living room develops, it gives me the greatest thrill of my life . . . ."

The beauty of the living room developed slowly and not without incident. Besides his trouble with the unit-system

and the location of the two piers, Hall contended with a chimney mass of unusual complexity and with masons who still failed to grasp what Wright expected; some of their stonework grew appallingly out of character, and had to be done over. Yet the wonder is not that mistakes were made, but that the house got built at all. Mosher had worked four weeks at Bear Run without a builder, and now Hall worked six weeks without a clerk-of-the-works. Construction continually fell behind schedule, usually without good excuse. Hall waited two weeks to pour the second floor because the plumbing, heating and electrical details still had to be worked out. Even window openings were revised, and, at Kaufmann's request, a radiator in his wife's bathroom was relocated so it could be built into her dressing-table. Hall at last could write on October 1:

I had a very hard day, pouring the second floor. Between rain and local laborers, at times I didn't know whether I was coming or going . . . .

I don't believe Mr. Kaufmann can make many more changes; also I have less need of one of your boys . . . .

Give me a sketch of the new arrangement and change of Junior Kaufmann's room, so that we can arrange the plumbing and heating. I received your sketch of the stairway, and believe it will be very nice.

Edgar Tafel, the apprentice Wright sent to Bear Run to resume supervision, was energetic, fun-loving and fond of the piano, although he played it much to the displeasure of Gurdjieff, the mystic friend of Mrs. Wright's. As soon as he got to Bear Run—it was October 7—he telegraphed Wright: "House wonderful. Will phone you tonight. Have plans at phone."

Tafel found the formwork for the second-floor slab still in place. The floor would be finished at nine feet two and one-half inches above the first floor; but because much of the terrace floor would be two feet one and a half inches deep, the ceiling at the south side of the living room would be only seven feet one inch high. But a different aspect of the second-floor slab affected the room more significantly. At the east corner of the room the slab reached well beyond the parapet of the second-story terrace. Perforated by a series of eight large openings, it was transformed halfway into a skylight and the other half into a horizontal trellis [38]. "Ceilings will often become as window walls," Wright said.[12] The trellis beams were slightly wedge-shaped, in answer to the shape of the bolsters, and they cast lively sun-splashes into the room. Another trellis, near the entrance loggia, performed a structural function by stretching across the drive to tie the second-floor cantilevers into the stone outcrop [39]. Two of the beams arced around trees that were growing close by the walls of the house [40].

Tafel sent his first report on October 9:

---

[12]Wright, *An Autobiography*, p. 340.

OPPOSITE, TOP: 38. Skylight and trellis.
ABOVE: 39. Trellis over drive. (Ezra Stoller © ESTO.)
OPPOSITE, BOTTOM: 40. Beam curved around tree.

41. Beam structure in west-bedroom terrace, December 1936.

I am about as good a typist as a speller, so will gain in the long run by writing it all out. Hall's secretary-cook-chambermaid is always busy making a completely canned meal in the kitchen, and isn't much of a help for typing.

Mr. Kaufmann is very pleased with the house. He debated the tunnel [the proposed bridge over the drive to a future servants' wing] and I explained it in detail, but he was sure he wants to do it sometime later, perhaps in the Spring. He told me about the general condition of the procedure: up to the time Bob left, Hall didn't bother to read the plans. Hall says so too; when no one was here to interpret them, Hall went to it and first learned about the building. Kaufmann said it was best for Hall that nobody was here. I think so too, only that in a few places we might have saved a few slight errors . . . but in general it's swell—parapets are true and level, and the heights are all there. However, the concrete does look heavier than it need be. I mean those joists that are 5″. The carpenters have the sheathing up for Mr. Kaufmann's terrace, and getting up high there the trees won't space out

evenly with the cantilever (concrete) beams. I've juggled them a bit to work out, and tomorrow we're to have a pneumatic drill to cut slots in the boulder . . . .

Tafel had to remove a tree to make way for the cantilevered west bedroom terrace, which would be five steps, or more than three feet, above the second floor. Wright wanted the other trees left free to rise *through* the terrace in witness to the marriage of house and site. The structure of the terrace slab entailed a single longitudinal beam, a foot and a half wide, and six narrower transverse beams. Box-like appendages allowed the trees to pierce the terrace, and three of the transverse beams keyed directly into the boulder, with reinforcement bars bent into lead anchors in the rock [41].

Kaufmann now got another idea. He had been sitting on the hill to study the west terrace, and he thought its parapet should end about nine feet from the west corner, to keep the terrace from looking "boxy, floppy and not at all

42. Second-story stone masonry, October, 1936.

strong." Tafel was diplomatic. "I really feel that Mr. Kaufmann's suggestion for his terrace change doesn't fit in so well," he wrote Wright on October 12. Wright responded by writing on the drawing: "What's wrong with boxy?" Then, more seriously: "Parapet must continue or entire construction will look disintegrated—F. Ll. W."

Late in October, the New York architect and planner Henry S. Churchill, a friend of Wright's, traveled to Bear Run and took a series of photographs that recorded the house under construction [42, 43]. Wright also visited Bear Run toward the end of the month; he was eager to retrieve Tafel. He found that the west bedroom terrace, the third floor and the roofs remained to be poured. More important, Wright learned of a new problem. Tafel stayed at the site and wrote Wright on October 30:

I have watched the two cracks, and tried by going over the construction with Mr. Hall to find some clue. This may have some bearing on the trouble: the four mullions that rest on

the living-room parapet were designed to be welded at tops, in two pairs. Mr. Hall tried saving the welding expense by just placing the horizontal "T" over the mullions. This may be perfectly all right, but one day last week I saw two men pounding at one of the mullions—it wasn't straight . . . .

Mr. Thumm noticed the checks, looked official and said he'd think it out, but I've heard no solution. After you left I checked over all the beams for size, and they check with the drawings.

The mistake of the extended slab past Mrs. K's terrace has been chopped back, and we are adding the extra amount over the stationary window in the living room, as it was originally designed . . . .

The cracks that Thumm pondered were in the second-story parapets. Wright wrote on November 2 to allay any worries Kaufmann might have, and he challenged Thumm's authority once again:

43. Formwork under cantilevers, October 1936.

Perhaps you don't quite realize the nature of what is being done for you and still imagine it could have been done without error or waste . . . Hall is doing remarkably well with awkward material.

By the way, just what is Thumm's relation to you where you are concerned with this building? . . .

I had the option of cutting through joints at the bearings of the concrete masses or taking such checks as might appear. I decided against joints in the faces of the cantilever masses as absurd to look at. A cantilever jointed over soffits is a kind of anomaly . . . .

And I hoped that the dampness in the glen and the slow curing of the concrete mass might minimize the inevitable and we *might* not have them to deal with. But all concrete structures do have them and are not at all weakened by them. But they give rise to head shakings by the ignorant . . . Have no concern about them yourself . . . I have a remedy that will eliminate them from sight although they must go on working forever.[13]

[13]Wright had used expansion joints in the upper walls of the Imperial Hotel, in Tokyo, but expressly to combat the racking movements of earthquakes. See Robert Kostka, "Frank Lloyd Wright in Japan," *Prairie School Review* III (3rd quarter, 1966), p. 17.

Hall had poured the roof over the guest-room terrace on October 29, and it was quick to show signs of distress. Tafel remained at the site longer than he expected to, and well into November; he saw the pouring of the west bed-room terrace, and saw the walls rise into the third story [44]. He can remember well his weeks at Bear Run:

During my time, we framed the ceiling above the master bedrooms, and then the roof above that. I remember the cement-mixer—a single-motored job, where every bit of sand, cement and gravel was shoveled into it. When mixed, it would be lowered into a wheelbarrow and hand-pushed to the location and "dumped" into the forms . . . into the parapets it had to be shoveled by hand. When the concrete was set, the forms were stripped and work started right away to "smooth" down the places where the form joints were, and a thin mix of cement was troweled on. That's why there's so much trouble with the parapets—the round tops were always crooked, and needed work. But at the end it looked all so "modern" a material, as if it all came out of a machine!

I made up the payrolls each Thursday, took them to Kaufmann's [in Pittsburgh], where E. J.'s secretary would put the cash into little brown bags, with the names of the workers.

44. Third-story stone masonry, November 1936.

45. Stone support for roof slab.

Deer season started exactly when we were to pour the second-floor roof slab, and nobody appeared on the site until each one got his deer. That delayed things several days only.

Mr. Wright wanted me back, and E. J. wanted me to stay on the job. I was happy to leave. It was cold [and] a lonesome place, with nobody around after working hours.

When he returned to Taliesin late in November, Tafel left Hall again on his own. Hall worked slowly, but reported to Wright on November 30 that Kaufmann was pleased with the progress and with the beauty of the design. "The workmen I have had on this house have been very unusual," Hall wrote, "staying home to gather crops, hunting and retaining their rights on government work."

Wright was becoming concerned about the cracks, and he wanted Hall to take levels on the parapets, on Mrs. Kaufmann's terrace and on the ceiling of the living room. The data were to be sent to Mendel Glickman. "We are trying to locate the exact cause of the cracks," Tafel wrote Hall on December 1. Hall responded two days later:

A new crack appeared, same as the others, in the parapet wall in left hand corner of guest bedroom. This is directly over the stone wall underneath. In my opinion there should have been expansion joints at these bearings. I have done this on bridges. These cracks mean nothing in my opinion . . . .

Wright also wanted to see the drawings by Metzger-Richardson for the first-floor slab and the roof above the guest-bedroom terrace. The stresses in the roof, the engineers found, exceeded "the allowable by a wide margin." Wright proposed a support—what Thumm described as a "concrete bolster": a row of steel rods through a vertical panel of concrete perforated by what Tafel has called a moon window. Kaufmann considered the concrete feature too fanciful, and without relation to the rest of the house. Hall installed the rods, and Wright suggested that they be strengthened with more steel and encased in channels. Finally, in 1937, the steel screen was replaced by a stone wall four feet nine inches long and a foot and a half wide [45]. It was not conspicuous, but it looked like a small pier that strangely hovered in space. "It just didn't belong," Tafel has said, "and we all knew it."

Soon the cracks began to multiply, and to weigh heavily on Hall. He reported on December 7:

On coming on the job this morning I discovered a new crack that took all the pleasure I have had out of this job away from me. On further investigation I found other cracks that came since the posts were taken out Saturday [December 5]. That really means there is something wrong . . . .

I have always had a habit of aligning horizontal and vertical lines with my eye regardless of level or plumb. This has been quite a satisfaction in casting my eye over the various lines. But now in doing this from the bridge it is very evident that terrace parapet falls 1″ below hatch parapet. This is my best reason for stating it is settling. I am so upset . . . .

Hall's letter arrived just as Wright fell gravely ill with pneumonia. Wright refused to go to a hospital. Mosher stayed at his side as he lapsed into the delirium of fever, and heard him mumble that Fallingwater was "too heavy." Kaufmann was anxious to confer with Glickman about the house; he called Glickman on December 11 and urged him to come to Pittsburgh as soon as possible. Glickman resisted. He wanted his directions to issue from Taliesin. Tafel wrote Kaufmann on December 14 that Wright was ill, and " . . . we cannot make this step without his consent." Kaufmann already had called Metzger-Richardson back to the site; on December 8 they made the first of what would seem an unending series of inspections.

The engineers found cracks in five places: the eccentric first-floor beam by the stairwell to the stream, the parapet at the stairwell, the concrete ribs of the east living-room terrace, the first-floor beam at the opposite side of the house and, on the second story, the parapet of Mrs. Kaufmann's terrace. All the cracks, they reported, extended through the members and would have to be considered structural. They blamed most of the cracks on excessive stress, but said that those in the second-story parapet—which worried Kaufmann the most—were due to the deflection of the first-floor slab. The remedies they proposed were all the same: an extension of direct vertical supports under all the cantilever beams and ribs deemed to be overstressed. Such, of course, would destroy the very nature of the house.

Wright recovered slowly, and came to think that the parapets added dead weight at the extremities of the cantilevers; later, he wrote that "next time, I believe, parapets will carry the floors—or better still we will know enough to make the two work together as one, as I originally intended."[14] Two days before Christmas, he asked Hall to cut out small blocks of concrete adjacent to fractures in five different areas of the structure, to mark the samples and to send them immediately to Taliesin. Hall reported the same day:

Mr. Kaufmann was out Sunday [December 20] and found a new fracture in the south parapet wall over center bolster beam. This is another proof that the southeast corner has gone down. I had seen the crack before but failed to show it to Mr. Kaufmann. He has taken this very calm considering

[14]Wright, in the *Architectural Forum*, 68 (Jan. 1938), p. 36.

the seriousness of it . . . I am dodging the facts to the workmen and outsiders until you can offer some solution. Mr. Kaufmann tells me not to worry, but as all I am getting out of this house is the happiness of building a Wright house, any failures hurt me to that extent.

In August, when he poured the first-floor slab, Hall had taken samples of the concrete and stored them in fruit jars; now Kaufmann balked at Wright's request for test cuts and further samples. Wright was strong enough to get angry, and he telegraphed Kaufmann:

Kindly refrain all interference with me in my work at this time. Send me what I ask for. I have no responsible representative in these circumstances. Easy to spoil the entire work by lack of confidence in my ability to handle my own work. Kindly stand by. Cut and send me the concrete samples as directed. They will not harm the structure. I will pay for them if in the outcome it seems necessary. I want an uncracked structure. Know how to get it. Intend to have it. Read my letter mailed yesterday. In circumstances like these there is only one doctor. Be thankful you didn't lose him. Now be good enough to realize the truth of what I say.

By the end of 1936 the shell of the new house on Bear Run languished under a palpable shadow of doubts [46]. It had been a long, hard year.

46. Construction view, December 19, 1936.

Finishing the House 1937

When he telephoned Wright the first day of the New Year and wrote the next day, Kaufmann expressed his concern for Wright's health. "All during your illness," he said, "something peculiar was affecting me. Take care of yourself—naturally, we are standing by."

Despite the trouble at Bear Run, all the mistakes, delays, lapses in communication, angry outbreaks and ominous signs of structural distress, Kaufmann sustained an extraordinary optimism, somehow greater even than Wright's. He telegraphed Wright on January 7 to share it:

> All is well. Sandoval arrived with helper this morning. Office will be constructed according to your latest plan. Cheer up, all difficulties must be overcome. Anxiously awaiting your solution as to what should be done because of the checks. Also your scheme to take the place of the masonry materials [gypsum plank specified for subflooring] and your authorization to start laying the floors in certain parts of the house. Those solutions all necessary for us to continue work during the winter . . . With all the difficulties it still remains a noble structure.

Carl Thumm, meantime, kept in touch with the engineers from Metzger-Richardson. Their calculations indicated stresses far in excess of the "allowable" in the main cantilever beam of the west bedroom terrace. In one of the changes Wright made after his early sketches, he greatly lengthened the terrace slab [47]. The terrace floor now extended 28 feet five inches. The engineers recommended that a four-foot stone wall be inserted under the slab to provide additional support. The wall was in place by January 4, Thumm noted, and two days later the engineers began loading all the cantilevered terraces to test their stability and to measure the deflections. They used 94-pound sacks of cement, 94-pound sacks of sand and five-foot lengths of cast-iron pipe that weighed 65 pounds each. With the new pier in place, they said, Kaufmann's terrace proved satisfactory; but when Wright learned about it—doubtless it was Hall who told him, later that month at Taliesin—he ordered the pier removed.

Wright wanted to talk with Hall about various details of the house and especially about the deflections of the cantilevers. He had decided to insulate and deafen the floors not with gypsum plank, but with redwood laid diagonally across the slabs, indoors and out—except in the kitchen, where the concrete floor was to be covered with red linoleum. To show Hall how to pave all the other floors he had made a tiny sketch of curved mortar in the joints between the flags. The roofs should blend in with the parapets, Wright said, and should have a thin coat of gravel "cream color to light gold" spread over the final coat of asphalt. Such was the discipline in his attention to detail.

Hall arrived in Wisconsin on January 23. Earlier that month, Kaufmann had left Pittsburgh on his winter vacation; he was in Palm Beach, Florida, when Wright first heard about the test-loadings. Wright sent a brief telegram on January 24:

> Are you prepared to take full responsibility for stability of concrete structure in view of tests you have conducted over my head?

Kaufmann immediately wired back:

> You must take full responsibility for stability of concrete structure taking into consideration the results of our tests. Same were made for additional data during your illness, after repeated attempts to have your engineer present.

OPPOSITE: 47. Cantilevered west-bedroom terrace. (Ezra Stoller © ESTO.)

Wright responded in a letter of January 25:

I suppose there is nothing in your experience by which you might measure the disappointment and chagrin which you have handed me. I have put my best inspiration and effort into creating something rare and beautiful for you, whom I respect and have conceived affection for, only to find that so far as you could add ruin to my work and reputation you did so behind my back when I was helpless, with no idea, apparently, that you were so doing (the reverberations have already reached me from New York City). Any pleasure I might take in having done something noble and fine for you is outraged by any outside interference with my effort on your behalf, no matter how well meant the interference may be . . . .

There is the work of art itself to consider. I will get on the job now that I am around again, issue the drawings and furnish the superintendence necessary to complete the work, but only on the fair conditions promised me when I undertook this unbelievably difficult work under all but impossible circumstances. And that condition is that the builder I selected to do the work be directly responsible to me . . . .

It never occurred to me that you had not enough common sense, when we set this up, to stick to it *through thick and thin* . . . I must ask for this reassurance from you—in writing this time—as necessary to your own interest as well as mine if this building is to be creditably finished.

. . . Hall is not the experienced builder I needed but he has muddled through pretty well, considering—though mixed up by your "Thumb" time and again. That should stop.

The scare over the integrity of the structure is the usual exaggeration where such matters go. I have assured you, *time and again,* that the structure is sound . . . Hall can now explain to you why the parapets cracked. And Hall himself crowned nothing in the building, as any experienced builder would have done to take up the inevitable 1″ to 1⅛″ deflection in cantilevers and beams given in all tabulations . . . .

Hall has now the thorough coaching he needs to go further with this work. Bob Mosher has been working under my direction on the details necessary to complete the work and is going back with Hall to await your decision in this matter.

Wright provided Kaufmann with a form to sign:

48. Three-story window with corner casements opened, late 1937.

I hereby agree to do all in my power to see that the architect's instructions to the builder, Hall, or whoever may take his place, agreeable to the architect, are faithfully executed and that no exterior advice or criticism be allowed to interfere with the architect's authority over matters concerning the character and integrity of the building I have engaged him to build for me. And this is to continue until the building is completed to our mutual satisfaction.

As if to give Wright further grounds for complaint, the roofing at Bear Run proceeded while Hall was in Wisconsin, and not according to specifications. But at least Wright secured his client's pledge. "I have your father's renewed assurance," he wrote the younger Kaufmann on January 28, "that he will do all in his power to see that my instructions to Hall concerning my work are carried out by him—and that I alone be responsible to him therefore." He asked the younger Kaufmann to make a friend, not an enemy, of Mosher. "You will find him posted and jealous of the honor of the work," Wright wrote. The reply from Edgar Kaufmann, jr., was tart: Mosher, he said, should at least try to understand the owner's viewpoint. Wright answered on February 1:

You mistake Bob's position somewhat. He is not there to adjudicate between owner and architect. He has no such power. He is there to interpret the architect's details and explain their intent and help to get them executed.

Any objection raised by the owner against those details comes to the architect.

Mosher and Hall returned to Bear Run in good spirits. "Bear Run is like a Hiroshige snow-print," Mosher wrote Kaufmann on February 4. A few days later, Hall wrote Wright:

I wish to offer my appreciation of the pleasant time I had at Taliesin. It will always be remembered by me. I am like the old fellow I knew who always dated things from the time he went to Niagara Falls. Bob's coming on the job has given it a new lease of life . . . The store crowd are naturally dying hard, but nothing but what we pass up good naturedly between Bob and I.

We located redwood and are right into the flooring business, the electric piping is all done and the plumber is finishing up the radiator work. The glass people are putting in glass . . . We are settling up the roofing contract and as soon as weather permits we will go ahead with suggested changes.

That same day, February 10, Kaufmann wrote Mosher:

In spite of having had a very pleasant and restful holiday, my thoughts have been daily, almost hourly, with the work in Bear Run, which has become part of me and a part of my life, and one hates to be separated until the work has been completed to everyone's satisfaction . . . Do not forget in drawing the details for furniture and woodwork that this is not a town house but a mountain lodge and should have that feeling in its furnishings . . . .

The pace at Bear Run remained slow. "The country and the country workmen are drawbacks," Mosher wrote Wright on February 11. "And the different trades work at the country gait, not their city quickness, except when it's time to quit." After months of discussion, Hope's Windows, Inc., of Jamestown, New York, had been chosen to supply the steel sash. All dimensions were to be taken at the site, not from the drawings, because of the revisions, deflections and deviations. The three-story window, installed in January, had enough steel in it, Mosher wrote, "to hold up that portion of [the] house." Traditionally, a window of that size would have lighted a staircase; but Wright's purposes were more fundamental [48]. To him, this was a great vertical light-screen: a shaft of glass that could manifest the rift between the stone mass of the chimney and the stone wall at the west side of the kitchen and bedrooms above [49]. The rift corresponded to that at the opposite

49. Rift between stone masses.

50. Window-wall at south side of living room.

51. Vanished corner.

side of the house, where the second-floor slab was perforated to form a trellis and skylight, and where the first floor was pierced by the stairwell to the stream. Wright meant to conquer every confining element of the building: not just the walls, but the ceiling and even the floor.

To the degree that he thought of the limpid surfaces of glass "playing the same part . . . that water plays in the landscape," all the light-screens alluded to the stream.[1] Wright found plate glass one of the marvels among modern building materials, its "crystal held by the steel as the diamond is held in its setting of gold."[2] Window-walls opened the house to countless perspectives across the glen; and to every vista the steel-sash members gave a rhythm and measure like that of a Japanese folding screen [50]. The sash bars also subverted humdrum post-and-beam construction; Wright withdrew the vertical members from the corners, and spaced the horizontal members on his 17-inch-unit system, as if in sideways mockery of wood studs. The glass at the corners was mitred and butted: The wraparound window, Wright wrote, was originally "a minor outward expression of the interior folded plane," an exponent of continuity.[3] In eight corners where there seemed to be mullions (in the kitchen and bedrooms above, near the dining table, at the stairwell to the stream, by Mrs. Kaufmann's dressing table, in the guest room and at the north corner of the second-story landing), small casements opened from both sides to astonish the eye by leaving no corner at all [51]. Wright expected to use special framing members where windows met the ragged profiles of stone walls, but Kaufmann said the glass could run directly into caulking channels, or chases, in the stone. This seemingly effortless penetration enhanced the character of each material by contrasting it to the other [52].

Hall put to work a full crew at the end of February to pave the floors with flagstones from the quarry on the hill. Indoors, the floors were to be sealed with two coats of shellac and one of Johnson's Wax to gain the same color and texture as the bedrock of the stream. Mosher expected to trim the boulder at the hearth: the working drawings showed it flush with the finished floor. Kaufmann suggested instead that it be left undisturbed, to rise through the floor as powerful testimony to the site. "E. J. ruled the day," Mosher recalled, "and that wondrous rock stayed untouched to this day. Isn't that superb?" Wright was pleased. "Count one for you, E. J.," he said. The boulder

52. Glass into stone.

extended almost seven feet into the living room and at some points stood nearly 10 inches above the floor [53]. It pierced the floor like a rock that peered above the glistening water of the stream. It became one of the most memorable details of the house, and the ultimate witness to Wright's philosophy that "it is in the nature of any organic building to grow from its site, come out of the ground into the light—the ground itself held always as a component basic part of the building itself."[4]

Long before the house was finished it began to attract publicity. In March the *St. Louis Post-Dispatch* reproduced in color the handsome rendering Wright had finished with Jack Howe standing at his side. In an interview, Wright gave the impression—quite exaggerated—that he had directed Kaufmann's attention to the waterfall site, saying:

[1]Wright, "In the Cause of Architecture: Standardization, The Soul of the Machine," *Architectural Record,* 61 (June 1927), p. 480.

[2]Wright, "In the Cause of Architecture: The Meaning of Materials—Glass," *Architectural Record,* 64 (July 1928), p. 12. Glass has a rich history of meanings; *see* Rosemarie Haag Bletter, "The Interpretation of the Glass Dream—Expressionist Architecture and the History of the Crystal Metaphor," *JSAH* XL (Mar. 1981), pp. 20–43.

[3]*Frank Lloyd Wright on Architecture,* ed. Frederick Gutheim (New York, 1941), p. 181. Wright achieved continuity in glass as early as 1924–25 in his house for Samuel Freeman, in Los Angeles.

[4]Wright, *An Autobiography,* p. 338. Having seen the drawings but not the house, John Lloyd Wright assumed that the boulder was "sheered flat"; see *My Father Who Is on Earth,* p. 124. Despite all the testimony to the contrary, Edgar Kaufmann, jr., in later years grew strangely reluctant to give his father credit for the idea of leaving the boulder alone.

53. Boulder at hearth. (Ezra Stoller © ESTO.)

You love this waterfall, don't you? Then why build your house miles away, so you will have to walk to it? Why not live intimately with it, where you can see and hear it and feel it with you all the time?[5]

Wright also said the house would cost $45,000 and its exterior concrete surfaces would be finished with gold leaf, the quiet gold of Japanese screens.

But he was overly sanguine on both counts. The costs would total nearly $75,000 by the end of the year, and from 1938 through 1941 more than $22,000 would be spent on additional details and for changes in the hardware and lighting. The servants' wing and guest suite, begun in 1939 and almost finished by the end of that year, would cost almost $50,000 more. The sums probably included payment for what Hall called the "store crowd": Thumm and other employees such as A. E. Vitaro, the store architect, who made some of the shop drawings. Some idea of the great expense of the house on Bear Run can be gained from the fact that Hall once wrote he was paying the laborers only 25 cents an hour. In short, Wright gave Kaufmann just about all the house he could get away with, and far more than the "waterfall cottage" they first discussed. His fees, however, proved fairly modest. They came to only $8000.[6]

As to the gold leaf, seemingly a fantastic proposal, Mosher recalled that Wright thought the moisture of the glen would transform it with a soft and rich patina, a shimmering autumnal cast perfectly at home in the forest. Despite his pronouncements on the color red, Wright had praised gold even more. "He says that yellow is the color of creation, of the earth, of life, of death; gold is the highest life and blessedness after it," Erich Mendelsohn wrote after he visited Taliesin in 1924.[7] Kaufmann nevertheless thought gold leaf extravagant, and inappropriate for a mountain lodge. He asked Mosher as early as August 1936 to inquire about "any new developments concerning foil for concrete." The process of reaching a decision took more than a year. Wright priced gold leaf and aluminum leaf that

September, but in March 1937 suggested a mica-white finish from Super Concrete Emulsions, Ltd., a Los Angeles company he soon visited. Kaufmann protested that the finish ought to blend with the stonework; so Wright sent a sample in what he called the key "of the sere leaves of the rhododendron." In truth, the leaves stay green through every season; perhaps he was thinking of fallen leaves. He had stained the outer walls of his Hollyhock House, on Olive Hill, to a light gray-green meant to echo the subtle tint of olive leaves. "Cemelith," a waterproof cement paint from Super Concrete Emulsions, was chosen in August; in September the color still had to be settled. The order came to 1340 pounds—and in a color, finally, that Kaufmann described as a light ocher.

Toward the end of March the deflections of the first-floor cantilevers were measured again, but not carefully. Wright was at his desert camp in Arizona when Mosher on March 27 sent him a diagram that reported deflections of more than two inches in both living-room terraces. Kaufmann received the same data from Hall, and it must have increased his anxiety. Where repairs had been made in the parapets of Mrs. Kaufmann's terrace, moreover, the cracks had opened again. Mosher was more occupied with the slow paving of the floors, not yet complete, and a host of other details that seemed forever in discussion:

The living-room floor was completed the night before the Kaufmanns arrived and the next morning they came in stomping off the heavy snow, surprised and pleased with the results. We are still quarrying; that has been a drawback, as the supply has had a hard time keeping up with the demand. We have replaced a number of spots done at the beginning in order to improve the whole. The stone has been thin and warpish, there are places I am not satisfied with, and I have taxed the stonelayers' patience to a high degree in making them replace, recut, and choose their stones. They are trained now but some have quit because of their lack of patience.

Mosher took pains to have the flags placed so the joints would appear to continue beneath the glass doors, to unite indoors and out. He was still waiting for Hope's to deliver the special hatch assembly, composed of glass gates and a telescoping glass roof; when the hatch was installed, in the middle of April, the house at last was closed in [54, 55]. Mosher was also concerned about painting the steel sash and the other metal details: the streamlined shelves, the stair hangers and railings, the fireplace equipment and all the flower boxes at the south side of the living room, hatch, second-floor landing and third-floor gallery. Wright specified Duco, which Mosher thought could not be applied with a brush, although advertisements even in the 1920s showed it being hand-painted onto furniture. Wright asked the Du Pont Company of Wilmington, Delaware, to mix the paint to a "Cherokee red." He sent along an Indian pot as a color guide, although the hue was like that of the bricks

[5]Max Putzel, "A House That Straddles a Waterfall," *St. Louis Post-Dispatch* Sunday Magazine, March 21, 1937, pp. 1, 7. In a discussion on May 31, 1974, Edgar Kaufmann, jr., noted an irony in Wright's siting of the house. Walking to the falls, he said, had been an excursion and special event: "Yet, as soon as the family began to live right above the falls, the urge to go down and make use of [them] lessened. It was an excursion no longer, it lacked the accent of effort."

[6]A copy of the capital-investment accounting undertaken after Kaufmann's death in 1955 is in the Avery Library. Wright's house of 1936–37 for Herbert Jacobs in Madison, Wis., cost only about $5500 including the architect's fee; *see* Herbert Jacobs with Katherine Jacobs, *Building With Frank Lloyd Wright* (San Francisco, Calif., 1979). "The house of moderate cost," Wright wrote in *An Autobiography*, p. 489, "is not only America's major architectural problem but the problem most difficult for her major architects."

[7]*Eric Mendelsohn: Letters of an Architect*, ed. Oskar Beyer (London, 1967), p. 72. Wright installed Japanese screens at Taliesin and in the Aline Barnsdall house ("Hollyhock House") in Los Angeles. In the Henry J. Allen house in Wichita, the Martin house in Buffalo and the Imperial Hotel he used gold mortar beds to accentuate the horizontal and to visually lighten the masonry masses. Gold leaf could have served the same purposes at Bear Run.

54. Hatch, late 1937.

OPPOSITE: 55. Hatch opened.

56. Metal shelves, late 1937.

he had chosen for the Johnson Wax Building. Characteristically, he used a product of modern technology to convey historic and even primal associations: red in homage to the Indian, red as an earth-color and symbol of the lifeforce (the idea he attributed to Timiriazev) and, as Edgar Kaufmann, jr., remarked, red as the sign of fire in the working of metals.[8]

Drawings were not finished until May 26 for two metal details Mosher mentioned in his letter of March 27, the streamlined shelves and the spherical kettle at the hearth.

The shelves could easily be mistaken as a 1930s cliché, but they in fact performed expressive functions specific to the house on Bear Run [56]. They echoed the rock ledges and concrete cantilevers; their rounded corners reiterated a subordinate theme of the house, and, in coursing along the upper wall, they modulated transitions from wall to ceiling and from one material to another.[9]

The kettle was a more curious detail, proposed by Wright for heating wine over the fire, a celebration of the primitive nature of the hearth [57]. Almost two feet across,

[8]In writing of his early years in Adler & Sullivan's offices atop the Auditorium Tower, in Chicago, Wright recalled how "the red glare of the Bessemer steel converters to the south of Chicago thrilled me as the pages of the Arabian Nights used to do—with a sense of terror and romance." See *Architectural Record,* 63 (Apr. 1928), p. 350. His notion of Cherokee red may have come from the color of the soil in what once was Indian Territory; his house of 1928–29 for Richard Lloyd Jones was built in Tulsa, Okla.

[9]The house presented a rare instance of streamlining in immediate relation to a stream. Norman Bel Geddes, who claimed to have designed the first streamlined ocean liner in 1928, wrote that in 1933 the word "streamline" was seized upon by advertising copywriters "as a handy synonym for the word 'new,' " although it ought to signify "the use of forms which reduce air resistance." See the *Atlantic Monthly,* 154 (Nov. 1934), pp. 553–554. Long before the fashion for streamlined moderne, Wright pursued the horizontal as an expression of shelter and expansive freedom.

57. Crane and wine kettle.

58. Outdoor stairs.

it was made of cast iron three-eighths of an inch thick. Despite the appeal of this ample vessel, it hardly served its ostensible function. Edgar Kaufmann, jr., recalled it being used only once, and only after a wine punch had been preheated in the kitchen. The great red sphere swung on a welded crane—another cantilever—and came to rest in a semicircular niche in the stone mass. Wright revised the back wall of the fireplace so it too would be semicircular: a response to the parapet by the hatch, diagonally opposite. Other arcs, at smaller scale, would occur in details of the furniture and in the stairs to the stream, as well as those added by Wright to give the Kaufmanns a way from the second story to their morning tonic, the plunge [58].

Too many details remained in abeyance; Wright was dilatory and Kaufmann could be as obstructive as he was creative. Many months passed before the plunge got built. Kaufmann had objected that it should be widened to ac-

commodate his breaststroke, or what Mosher called his "wingspread." Much more troubling, Kaufmann failed to see any reason for the hanging stairs to the stream. Wright finally sent a telegram, on April 2:

> Hatch has no meaning without intimate relation by stair to stream. Sure you will appreciate steps after living in the house awhile. Consider this feature absolutely necessary from every standpoint.

Edgar Kaufmann, jr., helped convince his father, while Mosher hastened to explain his own position. "I did not ask if the hatchway stairs could be omitted," he wrote Wright. "Their function to the house has always been clear in my mind . . . ." Surely that function was more aesthetic than practical, although the opened hatch helped ventilate the living room. To look through the hatch and down the stairs was to apprehend how bravely the house took its

59. Stairs from living room. (Ezra Stoller © ESTO.)

place above the stream. The stairs were an abstraction of the waterfall, and they cascaded in the opposite direction as a graceful but emphatic gesture of balance, of counterpoint [59]. The bottom step was eight feet wide, nearly three times the width of the steps to the plunge [60]. The hatch and hanging stairs had appeared in Wright's earliest sketches: He wanted the house above all to "associate directly with the stream."

Hall was taking time away from the building site, Mosher wrote, to work on his inn at Port Allegany. Mosher grew discouraged:

> The conditions have not been good . . . Hall has not been so much help and I have had to stand a good deal of it alone, which may have only added to my incapabilities. He complained always of not being well, and Taliesin spoiled him, as he has thought of nothing but trying to incorporate its ideas into his own building. He has left every weekend . . . his mind has not been here . . . .
>
> He left yesterday, I was unable to keep him here; he returns at the end of the week . . . .

Hall had written Wright on April 2 that he hoped to spend a month preparing his inn for lease on May 1, and that he would return to Bear Run when more materials arrived. He wrote again on April 26:

> From the standpoints of personal interest and financial welfare I am compelled to drop out of the picture as far as the Kaufmann house is concerned, unless the job can be shut down until Mr. Kaufmann, Mr. Thumm and Junior get together and decide on the color of the plumbing fixtures, etc., etc.
>
> Frankly, I've lost a lot of interest in this job. Mr. Thumm got off to a bad start with you and after bungling the stone quarrying and making a failure of his inspection of the bridge he became very embittered at my comparatively successful operations under similar conditions. He soon fell into the habit of sending men out whose minds were poisoned toward the job, one after another of these workers referring to it as a lot of damned foolishness.
>
> This was bad enough, but there has been a continual and unrelenting barrage of criticism both direct and indirect from Mr. Thumm and Junior. They were both quite disappointed at the outcome of my trip to Taliesin . . . Mr. Kaufmann is all right except that he is naturally the victim of his advisors.
>
> Perhaps you do not realize the punishment they have given Bob. At my size, I haven't had to take so much directly. But Bob, in his loyalty to you, thinks that he has to.
>
> Several times when things got too discouraging I have tried to quit, but each time Mr. Kaufmann persuaded me to stay . . . I wonder if Michelangelo had more trouble with the Pope than that we have caused you in the building of this house. My only regret is not the Kaufmann house but rather a desire that I could have been with you twenty years ago. Perhaps you could have made something of my native ability at a more plastic age . . . .

As if to compound the troubles at Bear Run, the engineers from Pittsburgh returned on May 21—by then the floors were entirely finished—to take "final elevations" of the sagging cantilevers. They wanted to compare the deflections due to the total dead load with those measured during the test loadings in January; they confirmed that the greatest deflections were in the living-room terraces, although at no point did a deflection exceed one and five-sixteenths inches. In a report signed by F. L. Metzger, the senior partner, and submitted on June 1, they reached a conclusion by now all too familiar to Kaufmann:

> The calculated stresses in the structure do not fall within the limits of those prescribed by accepted engineering practice. From this standpoint, therefore, the structure does not have a satisfactory factor of safety, or what might be termed reserve strength. We believe the recommendations we made from time to time, regarding the extension of supports at different points, should be carried out.

Although the climate and the nature of the house meant that it would always be slightly in motion, Kaufmann for almost 20 years had engineers travel to Bear Run to mea-

60. Steps from hatch.

61. Entrance loggia. (Ezra Stoller © ESTO.)

sure the deflections. Their record was plotted on graph paper, and the number of points on which they took readings grew from 14 to 35. Wright had proved superfluous the wall that stood so briefly under the west bedroom terrace; after that, Kaufmann refused to build any further supports recommended by the engineers. He stood fast by the house, and except for the roof above the guest room terrace and the trellis above the east living-room terrace, the house stood fast by him.

Hall's absences from Bear Run gave Thumm the opportunity to reassert what Wright considered his impudent interference. On one of his unwelcome letters, Wright simply wrote "The traitor." But at least Mosher was beginning to appreciate the contributions of the younger Kaufmann.

"Junior has been a good help in working out all the private requirements (shirt trays, etc.) for wardrobes and the general habits of the family built into the various rooms," he wrote Wright. "Routine of servants, kitchen and dining equipment, etc." Mrs. Kaufmann also attended to interior details; she was an experienced buyer for the department store. But when she sent Wright fabric samples, he politely demurred. The material should have a coarse texture and no pattern at all, he wrote her on June 6: "Because the environment is so rich and lively the detail of the furnishing can be merely tributary . . . I am afraid of more pattern as we have already put so much design into the thing."

Through the rest of 1937 the work went very slowly. "You seem to have forgotten your creation at Bear Run,"

Kaufmann telegraphed Wright early in September. Wright responded: "Forgotten the creation at Bear Run? Never."

Even the slightest decision demanded thorough consideration and discussion. Thumm sent to Taliesin a sample knob for the cabinet doors; and, on September 27, wrote Wright to remind him: "Will you please let us know by return mail whether or not this knob meets with your approval." With such patient attention to detail, the house could sustain its essential character at every turn. Its abiding sense of shelter and seclusion, and still gracious invitation, was expressed from the beginning, at the loggia and entry [61]. Stone, concrete, steel and glass met in perfect harmony, and without compromise. Inside, the walls parted in nearly every direction to become discrete supports, dispersed asymmetrically and as if by some inner centrifugal force—a pattern manifest in the floor plan. Straight ahead, a built-in table and shelf nestled against the stairs to the second story [62]. To the right, the walls opened to a coat closet and tall casement; to the left, three broad steps led up to a music alcove, the first of the distinctive areas of the living room [63].

RIGHT: 62. Desk by entrance.
BELOW: 63. Music alcove. (Ezra Stoller © ESTO.)

64. Double-cushioned ottomans.

"The Kaufmanns have purchased their sound recorder," Mosher wrote Wright on May 25, "which will just fit into the deep case at the seat near the entry; that is, if you think that is a good position." He was talking about a Capehart record player. Edgar Kaufmann, jr., proposed that all the special seat cushions be made of "Dunlopillo," a vulcanized liquid latex honeycombed with air bubbles, from the Dunlop Tire & Rubber Company of Buffalo, New York. The product had been introduced in buildings of a more public kind, such as hospitals, hotels, theaters and churches; and at the house on Bear Run it proved both durable and well ventilated. Some smaller cushions were covered in single-color red or yellow fabrics to form spots of brilliance against the gray sandstone floor and walls [64].

Beneath the skylight, next to the hatch, a second alcove afforded a place for reading and writing, and for the elder Kaufmann to conduct what Mosher called the Sunday morning "business conferences" [65]. In calculated contrast to the subdued light of the entry and music alcove, it was the brightest area of the room; it was also the point where sunlight and flowers, stream and forest, came so close together that the historian Talbot Hamlin soon pronounced it "perhaps the climax of the whole house" [66–68].[10]

The library table and bookshelves, in black walnut, were meant to be of ship quality to resist warping from the mois-

[10]Talbot F. Hamlin, "F. L. W.—An Analysis," Pencil Points, 19 (March 1938), p. 138.

ture of the falls. "E. J. thinks that walnut [is] too dark," Mosher reported on March 27, "but I said that a lighter wood would make everything too neutral in color, and that the contrast between the wood and stone would tend to make the stone appear lighter." He was exactly right. The millwork would figure large in the cost of the house, and Mosher tried for months to get on with it; not until June 4 did Wright get a bid from the Gillen Woodwork Corporation of Milwaukee, which he recommended as the best in the Middle West, though by no means the least expensive. George E. Gillen had been a vice president of Matthews Bros. Manufacturing Company, which so many years earlier was responsible for the millwork in the Darwin Martin house, in Buffalo. When the Matthews Company was sold at auction, early in 1937, Gillen reorganized the plant with many of the same artisans. One of them was Tony Prochaska, a Viennese, who took on the task of matching the veneers for Fallingwater.[11] Kaufmann let the contract on June 16, and Tafel went to Milwaukee on June 24 to visit the plant on North Port Washington Road and choose the flitches, or planks. He had written Mosher in February that the grain was to run horizontally in the wardrobes but vertically in doors, the edges of which were to be slightly beveled at 45 degrees. Tafel carefully selected flitches with sap streaks ("no wider than three or four inches," he wrote Kaufmann) to give flair to the flow of the grain. Wright loved wood as "the most humanly intimate of all materials" and he accepted veneers as a way of achieving continuity, of maintaining "the same flower of the grain over entire series or groups . . . as a unit."[12] He, too, visited the Gillen plant. One of the cabinetmakers, Arthur Cooley, could recall him many years later as an "eccentric" with a cane and a floppy hat. Gillen's contract comprised doors, cabinets, wardrobes, backboards for beds, built-in seats and desks, radiator casings, shelves and tables. Most of the millwork was shipped from Milwaukee in July and August.

The central open space of the living room, gently defined by the principal bearing points of the second-floor slab, was signified by an indentation of the ceiling [69]. Stepped back like the house itself, the ceiling hollow also functioned as an overhead light screened by a wood grille. Wright wanted to use Japanese rice paper in the screen, but he settled on beige muslin. In making layouts for furnishings more elaborate than the Kaufmanns were ever willing to

[11]See the Milwaukee Sentinel, July 18, 1937, sec. B, pp. 7, 9. Gillen also did the millwork in Wright's house for Herbert F. Johnson ("Wingspread") north of Racine, Wis. The company went out of business in Sept. 1941.

[12]Wright, "In the Cause of Architecture: The Meaning of Materials— Wood," Architectural Record, 63 (May 1928), pp. 481, 485.

OPPOSITE, TOP: 65. Living room, looking south. (Ezra Stoller © ESTO.)

OPPOSITE, BOTTOM: 66. Reading alcove, late 1937.

ABOVE: 67. Reading alcove, 1963. (Ezra Stoller © ESTO.)
OPPOSITE: 68. Opened hatch, 1963. (Ezra Stoller © ESTO.)

69. Ceiling light, looking north. (Ezra Stoller © ESTO.)

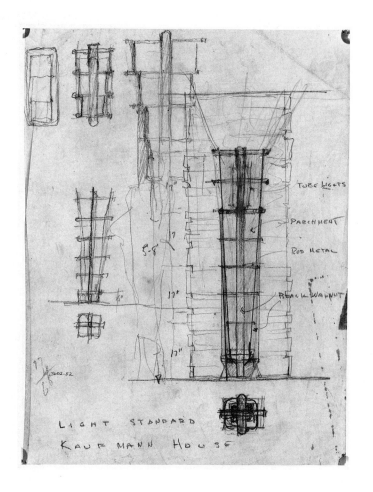

accept, he worked with small grid systems—somewhat as Japanese builders traditionally used the tatami mat as a floor module. A much smaller lighting screen, longer but very narrow, served the dining alcove. Mosher tried to have both screens made in Pittsburgh, but in the middle of September new drawings were sent from Taliesin to Gillen. Because the framing members were to be ornamented only sparingly with dentil bands, Gillen's bid of $714 seemed much too high, and Kaufmann demanded to be sent the drawings. "No client has a right to give orders over his architect's head," Wright wrote Gillen on October 2. He wrote Kaufmann on October 25:

> I met Gillen for the first time yesterday. He gave me a price of $600 on the ceiling light—but when you asked him for the drawings and a price direct . . . he added about $150 to get even with the scalping of the bid he gave on the house. It seems they lost considerable on the contract and are feeling a little sore . . . they figured too low to get it in the first place and then you made them feel they would lose it if they didn't come through the nose for another cut. He isn't complaining, exactly, but the situation now is such that I think you would better do the furniture yourself, so we are sending the drawings directly to you. Herewith. I had intended to ask them

OPPOSITE: 70. Alcove at west wall. (Ezra Stoller © ESTO.)
LEFT: 71. Sketch for living-room light standard.

for a price but if your own mill can beat them on the sky-lights, and the work is good enough, they can also beat them on these last items, I should think.

A built-in seat at the west wall focused still another al-cove, clearly a more convivial place than those at the record player and at the hatch [70]. But the longest seat ran all along the south window-wall, nearest the sound of the falls. Wright designed rugs for the living room—one would have been cut to fit around the boulder—but Kaufmann and his wife resisted formality in the house. In rejecting the designs, they gave their dogs as an excuse. Nor did they accept any of his designs for living-room lamp standards, or torchères [71]. Wright nevertheless fur-nished the room with six double-cushioned ottomans, six pedestal ottomans, four end tables (16 inches square), two coffee tables (five feet long and two feet wide) and the din-ing table (six and a half feet long and more than three feet wide, without its extensions). All answered to the horizon-tal thrust of the cantilevers and thus fit the house with ease and accord. From their old Aladdin cabin, the Kaufmanns brought in cocktail tables that were merely the inverted stumps of blighted chestnut trees. Because they suggested trees that grew upside-down, Wright disliked them. The room was also furnished with lounge chairs bought much earlier, in Berlin.

The most inward place of the living room, the dining alcove, was softly lighted from the small ceiling screen and

the high windows along the drive [72]. With its streamlined shelves and black-walnut sideboard so graciously occupied by vessels and plates, the dining area became a most gentle and endearing place. Wright wanted the chairs to be like those Gillen was making for "Wingspread," his overscaled house for Herbert F. Johnson near Racine, Wisconsin. They were a revised version of the barrel chairs he designed for the Martin house [see 79]. Instead, the family chose to use a group of three-legged Alpine chairs full of baroque curves. Mrs. Kaufmann bought them in Florence.

An opening in the west wall, fitted with small doors, formed a hatch to the kitchen, which was equipped in a straightforward way with St. Charles cabinets and an AGA stove, neither being intended to express the special character of the house [73]. Stairs at the west corner led down to the wine cellar and boiler room, the spaces Mosher had excavated with such difficulty from the midst of the boulders

so poorly represented on the plot plan. H. A. Thrush & Company of Peru, Indiana, supplied the oil-fired furnace and the forced-hot-water-heating system.

A stone stairway at the opposite side of the dining alcove led to the second-story landing, at three steps below the second floor—just as the entry was positioned three steps below the first floor. Indoors, the stairs were as concentrated as those outdoors were dispersed, and that made the landing an exceedingly complex space; virtually a pinwheel of passages in every direction [74]. To the east, a glass door opened to fresh air and the outdoor stairs to the living-room terrace, thence down to the plunge; or, alternatively, to three steps up to the guest-room terrace, sometimes called the sleeping terrace [75]. The landing also gave to steps up to the guest room and bath; to steps to the other second-story rooms and finally to the stairs to the third floor [76]. Later, it would open to the bridge over the drive.

OPPOSITE: 72. Dining alcove.

ABOVE: 73. Kitchen.

RIGHT: 74. Second-story landing, looking east.

If compared to the spacious and richly episodic living room, the bedrooms seemed small and simple; they were meant to serve almost as antechambers to their respective terraces, each of which offered more floor space [77].[13] From the years of the Aladdin cabin, the Kaufmanns were accustomed to sleeping on screened porches, and for a long time the elder Kaufmann entertained what he called his "bird cage idea" for screened sleeping on the terraces of the new house. He discussed it with Wright as early as April 1936. Later, he had a drawing made for a mobile steel-framed sleeping chamber—a scheme he abandoned only after a Pittsburgh manufacturer advised him in September 1937 that it could not make the contraption.

[13]Although the floor space of the living room is much greater than that of its two terraces, the total space in the house, about 2885 sq. ft., is not much more than that of all six terraces, about 2445 sq. ft. Mrs. Kaufmann's room, 14′11″ (E–W) by 17′, is 255 sq. ft.; its terrace, 685 sq. ft. Kaufmann's room, 12′2″ by 17′5″, is 210 sq. ft., the west bedroom terrace, 455 sq. ft. The guest bedroom, 11′5″ by 15′1″, is 172½ sq. ft.; its terrace 273 sq. ft. The third-story room, 11′4″ by 17′1″, is 192 sq. ft.; its terrace about 556 sq. ft.

OPPOSITE, TOP: 75. Guest-room terrace.

ABOVE: 76. Stairwell, with guest bath at left.

OPPOSITE, BOTTOM: 77. Terraces.

Wright's design, like that at the entry, and a barrel chair Gillen had made as a prototype for the dining alcove [79]. Tall casement windows at both east corners and two very small casements in the stone wall behind the bed helped ventilate the room.

Mrs. Kaufmann's bedroom was the largest of the upstairs rooms [80]. It opened onto the largest terrace, and it had the most commodious bathroom [81]. Most of all, however, it was distinguished by the beauty of its fireplace [82]. Three large stones sounded the theme of ledge and cantilever, and the hearth stepped back in quick returns that echoed the declivitous character of the site. The detail drawings for the fireplaces were made by Edgar Tafel. "The last of them designed—Liliane's—I did out of my own head, and worked it out at the quarry," he has recalled, "with changes to be done at the jobsite."

Kaufmann's room, of modest size, had an unmistakably virile energy generated by the vigor of its surfaces and variety of its wall openings [83]. The ceiling was held to one plane, but it followed an irregular plan of great dynamism, and the fireplace had a severe but majestic simplicity [84]. When it became apparent how much of the writing desk would be sacrificed to the radiator casing, Wright redesigned the desk to extend in front of the windows with a quarter-circle cutout to accommodate the inward swing of the tall casement [85]. He repeated the detail in the room directly above. For the wardrobes, Edgar Kaufmann, jr., proposed a scheme of sliding trays in walnut-framed cane, perforated for ventilation to avert mildew [86]. He also asked that the bathroom walls and floors be finished in cork—a softer, warmer, more strongly textured material than the usual ceramic tile [87, 88]. The corners, convex or concave, were to be curved as an expression of Wright's ideals of plasticity and continuity. Revised bathroom layouts were finished on May 24, and Mosher recalled how much trouble he had in achieving the curved surfaces; he called in representatives of the Armstrong Cork Products Company from Lancaster, Pennsylvania. But the elder Kaufmann was especially concerned with the bathroom fixtures. In a house so sympathetic to its site, he said, perhaps the tubs, basins and stools should be hewn from the native rock. Mosher, at first bewildered, soon interviewed tombstone carvers; the next weekend, he had only to compare their estimates to the cost of ordinary fixtures, and Kaufmann spoke no more about "indigenous" bathrooms.[14]

[14]The fixtures were from Kohler, in Kohler, Wis. Most of the toilet bowls were only 10½″ above the floor, thus sympathetic to the horizontal thrust of the house. They were sunk into hollows in the floor slabs at the direction of Kaufmann, who subscribed to a health fad that favored lower bowls as more "natural." Earl Friend, who began working at Bear Run in June 1936, has recalled that Kaufmann had a nail keg cut in half to demonstrate how high he wanted the bowls to be. In the later 1930s, Kohler began to produce a low 10″ bowl. Wright curved all corners in the bathrooms of the Imperial Hotel and tiled the floors of the hotel guest-wing corridors in cork.

From the configuration of the third-floor slab, the guest room and Mrs. Kaufmann's room gained a vital and characteristic change of ceiling heights. The slab was only eight and a half inches deep, and was folded for greater strength; that made the ceilings shift from six feet four and a half inches at the window-walls to a more generous seven feet nine and a half inches near the hallway. The lower plane inflected the sitting areas outdoors, the higher gave amplitude above the beds. Although nearest the stairs, the guest room provided great privacy [78]. It was in fact the only room of the house supplied with blinds: the thin wood slats of Aeroshades. The writing desk had another lamp of

78. Guest room.

79. Guest-room furniture.

81. Dressing table for Mrs. Kaufmann.

80. Mrs. Kaufmann's room, late 1937.

82. Fireplace, with late Gothic Madonna and child.

84. Fireplace detail.

83. Kaufmann's room.

85. Detail of desk.

86. Wardrobe detail.

87. Cork surfaces in bathroom.

88. Bathroom fixtures.

89. Third-floor gallery, looking east.

The third story consisted only of a bedroom planned for Edgar Kaufmann, jr., and a gallery that extended more than 26 feet to the east [89]. In 1939 the bridgeway to a new wing was built over the drive at the second floor only, and the gallery could have become a vestigial passage that led nowhere. But the elder Kaufmann had suggested as early as November 1936 that a bed might well fit into the small space east of the stairwell. This indeed became his son's bedroom, a cheerful alcove that caught the morning sun and opened conveniently to the long third-story terrace [90]. Now the room to the west became a study and dressing room [91]. An unusual reddish stone, discovered in the quarry, formed the mantel for its austere fireplace [92]. Beyond the study, a small balcony looked down on the west bedroom terrace, to which the briskly stepped staircase cascaded with staccato and comic vigor [93]. The west wall of the elder Kaufmann's room was to have opened with steps up to the terrace; but Wright shifted the doorway to the north end of the room, to make the path more subtle and indirect. The terrace overlooked most of the house [94].

On July 22, Mosher reported that the house was structurally complete, with its heating, plumbing and lighting systems in place, and the kitchen equipped. The bridge across the stream had been rebuilt to the same character as the parapets and walls of the house. Most of the metalwork and casework was well under way. Although the furniture would take many more months, the Kaufmanns began to use the house that fall. The costs already amounted to about $70,000—more than twice what Kaufmann had hoped to spend. In the letter he wrote Kaufmann on October 25, Wright described Taliesin as a "great extravagance," then refigured his fees and traveling expenses. He added $25 for each week an apprentice served as clerk-of-the-works; of that amount, Tafel has recalled, the apprentice was to receive only $12.50 and Wright was to keep the other half. And, as if by habit, Wright asked Kaufmann for more money:

knowing how a man feels when he is rounding up the costs on his home, I wouldn't ask for it just now.

But you got your money's worth out of an architect if ever a man did, and probably for the first time in your life?

N.B. All we need is one more commission into which I put as much of myself as I did into this one to go out of the picture here. When you begin to "sob" over the cost—just take a look at the drawings for the $35,000 house and . . . what it became because we "nursed it" to a conclusion . . . .

Kaufmann seems not to have answered "the sorrowful," as Wright was amused to call his plea for money, and he delayed paying the Gillen company. Instead, he wrote Gillen on December 1:

Since your work has turned out extremely unsatisfactory in the question of warping, I suggest that you satisfy yourself as to whether it is our fault or yours. I can assure you to the best

90. Third-floor terrace and clerestory over guest bath. Bronze sculpture is *The Harpists*, by Jacques Lipchitz, 1930.

ABOVE: 91. Entrance to study, looking west, with portrait of Liliane Kaufmann.

RIGHT, TOP: 92. Fireplace in study.

RIGHT, BOTTOM: 93. Third-floor balcony and staircase.

OPPOSITE: 94. View from west bedroom terrace, late 1937.

of our ability of judging, the warping is not due to any undue strain which has been put on the woodwork or by any physical conditions existing in the house.

Wright had recommended the Gillen company, so he came to the defense. Any masonry house, and especially the one at Bear Run, he wrote Kaufmann on December 19, could be expected to be damp before its first season of heating:

> Anyone knows that. Inevitably any woodwork will warp some if it is installed in a building before it has had a season of interior heat. Woodwork in a masonry house like the Bear Run house is never still. It will come and go somewhat for several years. Anyone knows that too . . . .

> To straighten warpage now would only result in warpage the other way then. To make such warpage the basis for withholding payment to a responsible concern for its work seems unfair. If the Gillen people are responsible (I believe they are) they will, next May or June, take care of any excessive warping . . . Kindly settle up with them, as I got them into this thing and their price for doing the work I believe [was] extremely small—as I believe also will be their costs for correcting the work they have done.

At the end of 1937 the house still lacked some furnishings. Kaufmann wrote to Taliesin about such items as bedroom rugs and the desk and bed lamps. By now the house was well into use as the family's weekend retreat. Edgar Kaufmann, jr., wrote Wright that "time is teaching all of us to like you in the house, and the house in us, more and more, so some inadequate personal thanks should be expressed for your weekly Christmas gift to us."

Liliane Kaufmann also took great pleasure in the house; on New Year's Day she wrote Wright to thank him for a Japanese woodblock print of irises he had sent as a Christmas gift:

> We have had the two happiest weekends of our lives in the house, the one over Christmas and this one. There are large balsam branches laid along the metal shelves around the living room and twined in the bars of the balustrade going up the staircase—you can't imagine how lovely it looks. We have had rather large house parties both weekends and it is a continual delight to see how beautifully the house adapts itself to large and rather scattered groups of people . . . We all three wish you the happiest of New Years and are more than grateful for the joy you have given us. [15]

[15] The woodblock print, Hiroshige's "Iris Garden at Horikiri," 1857, remains in her bedroom today.

The Servants' Wing, Guest Suite and After

Fallingwater entered the public imagination all at once, in January 1938. Early that month, the *Architectural Forum* devoted its entire issue to Wright's work. Wright designed the magazine and wrote the text. Fallingwater took a dozen pages, and the office interior in Pittsburgh took two more [95].[1] "The ideas involved here," Wright wrote of the house on Bear Run, "are in no wise changed from those of early work. The materials and methods of construction come through them, here, as they may and will always come through everywhere. That is all. The effects you see in this house are not superficial effects." A concluding phrase—"and are entirely consistent with the prairie houses of 1901–10"—did not quite fit on the page.[2]

By "superficial effects" Wright meant the look of European modernism, or the so-called International Style, which he considered two-dimensional and as inhibiting to freedom in space as to any true relation to nature. Exponents of that sort of modernism, he said, were as alike as peas in a pod: "All denying the pod though, and especially denying the vine on which the pod containing the peas grew."[3] Wright thus offered Fallingwater as an exemplar, just as he would write of the Johnson Wax Building as an "authentic example of Modern Architecture" in opposition to the skin-deep styling of international modernism.[4] He particularly wanted to say that the house was not an American response to European developments, but flowered instead from his own early principles and his own creative power, both of which had matured some three decades earlier. Later, he identified his house for Mrs. Thomas H. Gale, from around 1909, as the "progenitor as to general type" of Fallingwater.[5] He asked Jack Howe to restore an old perspective drawing of the Gale house, and to add the title "Oak Park 1904" along with the indication of a trellis cantilevered to the east, a feature that did not in fact exist either in the original drawings or in the house as built.

The portfolio in the *Architectural Forum* was promoted as "the most important architectural document ever published in America" and was intended to appeal to a public beyond the architectural profession. It was advertised on the inside

---

[1]Construction of the office began in Jan. 1937 and continued through July; the two rugs and the textiles for the furniture, handwoven in the studio of Loja Saarinen at Cranbrook, in Bloomfield Hills, Mich., were not shipped until Jan. 1938. Mrs. Saarinen, a sister of the architect Herman Gesellius, was the wife of the architect Eliel Saarinen and mother of the architect Eero Saarinen. Built of cypress hollow-core plywood from the American Plywood Corporation of New London, Wis., the office measured about 23′ by 26½′, with an eight-foot ceiling. Its principal feature was a "marquetry wall," or wood mural, in six stages of relief: a geometric abstraction related to Kaufmann's interest in Broadacre City and planned land use, such as that proposed by Stuart Chase in *Rich Land, Poor Land* (New York, 1936). The furniture included ottomans, chairs, a built-in seat, cabinets and a long desk with extensions. Edgar Kaufmann, jr., donated the office to the Victoria and Albert Museum in South Kensington, London, in 1974.

[2]Cf. *Architectural Forum*, 68 (Jan. 1938), p. 36, with the ms. version as published in *Frank Lloyd Wright on Architecture*, p. 232.

[3]Wright, *An Autobiography*, p. 304. The notion of an International Style appeared in F. S. Onderdonk, *The Ferro-Concrete Style* (New York, 1928) before it was promoted by The Museum of Modern Art in New York. Le Corbusier toured America in 1935 and a small exhibition of his work was held at the museum. Walter Gropius and Mies van der Rohe arrived in America in 1937.

[4]Lipman, *Frank Lloyd Wright and the Johnson Wax Buildings*, p. 182.

[5]*Sixty Years of Living Architecture: The Work of Frank Lloyd Wright* (Los Angeles, 1954), n.p. Despite his lifelong devotion to Wright's work, Edgar Kaufmann, jr., seems not to have grasped its basic continuity of expression. "Fallingwater was not much like the earlier architecture that had made Wright famous," he could write in *Fallingwater: A Frank Lloyd Wright Country House*, p. 28.

95. Office of E. J. Kaufmann.

front cover of *Life* magazine for January 17 with a dramatic photograph of Fallingwater from below the falls [96]. "I was thrilled when I saw this picture," Wright wrote when he mailed it to Kaufmann. "It surely means a new era in architecture." In his published commentary, Wright saluted Kaufmann as an intelligent and appreciative client. George Nelson, then an editorial associate of the *Forum*, has recalled working with Wright on the January issue:

> There is no doubt in my mind that for Wright the Kaufmann house was one of his great favorites, and I particularly remember the loving detail he would go into in describing how he developed the basic format and the details. For

Wright, Edgar Kaufmann was one of his truly great and favorite clients, and as far as I am concerned, this high regard was well placed. Kaufmann was a true merchant prince, a man of great personal power, full of what we have come to call charisma and possessed of a vision that is anything but common. In retrospect, I would say that they did very well by each other.[6]

The new house also appeared in the January 17 issue of *Time* magazine, both in a photograph and in the color rendering behind Wright's portrait on the cover. *Time* said the house on Bear Run was his most beautiful work.

[6]Letter of Dec. 31, 1973.

ABOVE: 96. Fallingwater, late 1937.

OPPOSITE: 97. View from bridge, late 1937.

Finally, a photographic exhibit devoted to the house was about to open at The Museum of Modern Art, in New York. John McAndrew, the new curator of architecture and industrial art, already had visited Bear Run in the fall of 1937, when it was also being photographed, at the request of the *Forum*, by Hedrich-Blessing of Chicago [97]. He had left a teaching position at Vassar College, where one of his students had been Aline Bernstein, who graduated in 1935. She and her brother, Charles Alan, a stage designer in New York, were related to Henry Kaufmann's wife; and that was how McAndrew got wind of the new house:

> I had heard from Charles Alan who had heard from "Uncle Henry" that the Kaufmanns had got Mr. Wright to build them a strange week-end house. I wrote the Kaufmanns and asked whether it would be possible for me to see it on the way back from Chicago to New York . . . and got back an extraordinarily nice letter from Mrs. Kaufmann explaining

that Bear Run was not in Pittsburgh but out in the country, and that the only way to see it would be to go for the week-end . . . .[7]

Impressed by the house, McAndrew began to plan an exhibit. Through the editors of the *Architectural Forum* he met Edgar Kaufmann, jr., who telegraphed Wright in Arizona to solicit his cooperation:

[7]Letter of Dec. 15, 1975. Aline Bernstein had met Edgar Tafel in the fall of 1936, when he went to Pittsburgh for the weekly payroll at Bear Run. As an art critic for the *New York Times,* she quoted Wright as saying: "We looked at the site of Bear Run, Pa., in 1936 [*sic*] and went home and made a drawing, and the building is almost exactly like it: Bear Run shows that buildings grow from their sites . . . ." See "Frank Lloyd Wright Talks of His Art," *New York Times Magazine,* Oct. 4, 1953, p. 27. Later that year, she married the architect Eero Saarinen. Edgar Kaufmann, jr., joined the staff of The Museum of Modern Art at McAndrew's invitation, and later served as director of the department of industrial design. He resigned in 1955.

Time is short . . . Setup is elegant. McAndrew wants future exhibits and seems sincere, much unlike his predecessors, which can help us lots.

"A New House on Bear Run, Penn., by Frank Lloyd Wright" opened January 24 in the museum's temporary quarters in the underground concourse of the former Time-Life Building, at 14 West 49 Street. The exhibit was composed of 20 photographs, and accompanied by a brief catalogue that reproduced some of the pictures along with the plans and elevations and the same commentary by Wright as in the *Forum*.[8] Edgar Kaufmann, jr., wrote Wright of the opening:

Business took me to New York the opening day of the Museum of Modern Art show, and I tho' you'd like to hear a little of it . . . Without a formal opening or anything but the slightest advance press notes, the crowd was steady and good. I found myself explaining away the misconceptions of journalists and journalistes, the latter the worse. The elder mesdames Rockefeller and Guggenheim appeared, asked some shrewd housewifely questions, seemed to appreciate the charm of the house and left. A Mrs. Hay, chairman of the advisory board, was quite enthusiastic. She was young. The total effect is strong and pleasant; I think you'd find it decent, tho' not in your manner; and much of the public, warmed up by the publicity in periodicals, will give it some study.

The enormously favorable publicity must have pleased Wright; he was in his seventy-first year, and the battle he was waging against the European modernists at last seemed to be going his way.

Characteristically, he had begun the New Year by asking his best client for more money. "Do not count on me," Kaufmann telegraphed on January 3. "Hope you can arrange with someone else." Kaufmann soon gave in, however, and wrote Wright on January 11:

Your reckoning and mine differ. Nevertheless, I will not let you down in spite of the house and furnishings still not completed.

Edgar Tafel spent the day with me yesterday and he promised to write you about the number of items that we are still awaiting answer from you. When you hear from him will you please not let me down and give me the answers as promptly as possible.

[8]The exhibit ran until March 1. The photographs were from Hedrich-Blessing of Chicago (taken after the formwork was removed at the end of October 1937), from Luke Swank of Pittsburgh, who was a friend of the Kaufmanns', and from McAndrew. Edward Alden Jewell reviewed the exhibit in the *New York Times* the day after it opened. Some of Swank's pictures appeared in the *Pittsburgh Post-Gazette* on Jan. 18 and in the magazine of the *Pittsburgh Press* on Feb. 6. The *Art Digest* of Feb. 1 mentioned the exhibit and the special issue of the *Architectural Forum,* and on Feb. 6 the gravure section of the *New York Herald-Tribune* published three of the Hedrich-Blessing photos. Lewis Mumford discussed the exhibit in *The New Yorker* of Feb. 12, and Talbot Hamlin discussed and illustrated the house in the March issue of *Pencil Points*.

I have a deep feeling for everything that you do in this world and my accounting with you will probably never be settled in dollars . . . I am mailing One Thousand Dollars.

Kaufmann was eager to add a servants' wing, carports and more guest rooms. He wrote Wright again on January 25:

I am enclosing [a] topography map, as well as Section A and Section B, showing the . . . condition of the rock where it is suggested the proposed gallery [a bridge over the drive] be built.

In planning the servants' wing, the following will be the requirements: 4 single bedrooms for servants, one bath. If possible, a combination kitchen, laundry and sitting room.

Naturally, the kitchen should be purely an emergency layout for such cooking as might be required when we are not there. The laundry equipment, both the washer and the mangle, could be rolled away into some compartment when not in use, and when there is no cooking and no laundry, the room could be used as a sitting room for the servants.

There should be a minimum space allowed for four cars to be stored, and we should like, if possible, to add two single and one double guest rooms and bath.

Although the servants' quarters and carports came first in his program, the new wing sometimes was called the guest house. "When do you want to build the extensions?" Wright asked in a letter of February 22, after waiting nearly a month to respond. "We will try to have the plans then." Kaufmann was in Sun Valley, Idaho, for four weeks of skiing. "In reply to your letter," he wrote on March 10, after he returned to Pittsburgh, "I would say as soon as the plans come to us we will start to break ground—so when can you start to work on them?"

Another month passed. "Anxious to go ahead with servants' house at Bear Run," Kaufmann telegraphed from Madison, Wisconsin, on April 11. He had just been to Racine, where he saw the Johnson Wax Building and the Herbert F. Johnson house under construction. "When can we expect plans? Answer Pittsburgh." The plans were finished by May 2 but to no result. Wright had failed to conceive the new wing with anything like the decisive integrity of the main house; the studies and preliminaries were in fact clumsy, even faltering. Nor did the working drawings show any improvement. The link to the main house entailed an enclosed pedestrian bridge 39 feet long—an awkwardly tunnel-like passage to a semicircular covered walkway—and the entrance to the guest rooms looked all too formal. The guest rooms gave to a gallery along the north side of the addition; the Kaufmanns were concerned about the lack of cross-ventilation. The entire scheme notably lacked Wright's characteristic subtleties. Kaufmann responded on May 31 as gently as possible:

We have been studying the plans for the extension at "Fallingwater" and we are very enthusiastic about them excepting that when discussing the matter further with Mrs.

Kaufmann I find she feels it will be too great a burden to put such a large addition on the present house. She is very anxious to keep it simple and with the least amount of care—so several other ideas have developed, which I believe we can only talk about if you could arrange to come and spend a day with us, which you promised to do that last time you were through.

Wright did visit Bear Run in the middle of June, but the rest of 1938 saw no progress beyond the changes, adjustments and additions to the details of the main house. Between the spring and fall of 1938 the architect Walter Gropius built a house for himself in Lincoln, Massachusetts, without any specially designed parts, and for only $18,000. Edgar Kaufmann, jr., was surprised to see that Gropius got better hardware from Hope's than had been supplied to Bear Run.[9] He complained to the company, and 10 more sheets of drawings were made between October 25 and December 2 for hardware improvements to the double outfolding doors to the terraces, the single side-hung doors, the casement screen doors and so on. Nine additional sheets were finished by January 14, 1939. Most of the screens had yet to be made. When they arrived at the house, the younger Kaufmann decided to leave them in the factory blue-gray finish, for contrast with the Cherokee red of the steel sash. "It was my hunch to leave them thus, without painting them red," he recalled in 1974. "When he saw the results, Wright approved the idea."

The first day of 1939 fired E. J. Kaufmann's resolve to build the new wing, and he thought again of Walter Hall in Port Allegany. Hall took great pride in the immediate renown of Fallingwater. The previous March, he had written Wright:

The presentation of Fallingwater has made me "homesick" (for lack of a better word!). It's on my mind constantly. Of all the pictures the oval view which appeared in the *Pittsburgh Press* pleases me most. It seems I never will tire of looking at it—a reality more beautiful than any painting I ever saw. It was a great privilege to assist in its construction. If I lose everything else I'll still have the happiness of that memory.

You once told me to take the work as a whole. I agree. All those daily irritations don't amount to much in light of the final result.

I regret that it has taken me so many years to begin to understand what you are diving [sic] at. My son is working hard to get it and I like to believe that he is . . . .

He wrote Wright again on January 5, 1939, to report his fresh contact with Kaufmann:

Last Sunday [January 1] I received a call from Mr. Kaufmann who asked me to come down for a conference on Wednes-

[9]In the Jan. 1938 issue of the *Architectural Forum,* Hope's advertised with a photograph of the corner drop-out windows: "The manufacture of this combination of steel casement windows, and of the many others which form such attractive details in this residence, called for special construction in our shops."

day. I immediately tried to call you at Taliesin for information and instructions, if any.

Being very busy, Mr. Kaufmann gave me only a few moments; handed me prints of the original guest cottage elevations and the revised floor plan, and suggested that I begin work this coming Monday [January 9] with a financial arrangement similar to the previous one.

After examining the prints and finding that they are undimensioned preliminaries, I am anxious to know how soon you can forward working drawings sufficiently advanced that the foundation may be placed.

I am quite happy to be able to resume this interesting job, and hope to make much better progress than on the original house. Plans, details and materials forthcoming (and the blessings of the weather man!) it shouldn't take long . . . In the few years left to me, I hope to build only those unusual and beautiful modern structures at which the average contractor balks.

Kaufmann on January 4 had voided the working drawings of the previous May, and on January 6 he wrote Wright that Hall was ready to go to work. "We are all thrilled that we are building again," he said. "It will help to fill up the first six months of 1939—so details are important. Please don't let us down—get to work!"

Wright was being rushed: not just by Kaufmann but by Hall, who arrived at Bear Run on January 10 and wrote him two days later:

Perfect summer weather. Seemingly having a free hand, placed 12 men to work quarrying stone. Staked out building and started grading terrace . . . Now to keep going if you could send rough detail of cross-section . . . I could be working on the walls while further plans are being made. I would like to clear up a feeling that might hang around Kaufmann's that it takes me too long to build anything. I see nothing about the plans that will be hard to work out after the experiences of "Fallingwater."

But there was another reason for the hurry, as Kaufmann wrote Wright on January 17:

On June 22nd of this year we will be married thirty years and although I have not said anything to Liliane, I would like very much to have the house completed and fixtured for that day. If you will cooperate with us I think I can speed up the work . . . .

Hall sensed the danger in his position between client and architect. He wrote Wright on January 19:

I now have about a hundred yards of excavating out and two thousand cubic feet of stone quarried.

I understand from the usual Sunday Conference [on January 15] that they are right after you for further plans . . . .

I wish to state right here that I am naturally playing the game with you, and they know it and wish to make me a go be-

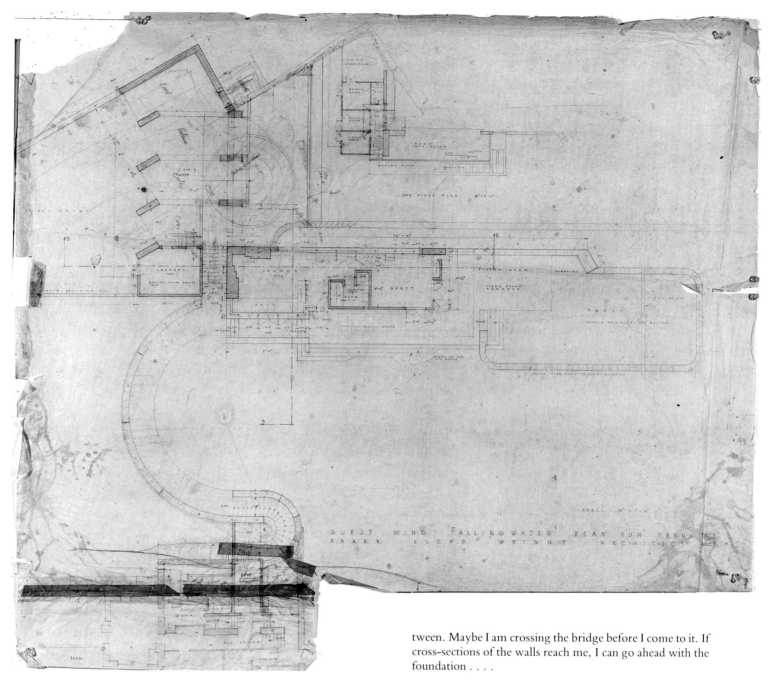

ABOVE: 98. Plan of servants' wing, January 1939.

OPPOSITE: 99. Elevations of servants' wing, January 1939.

tween. Maybe I am crossing the bridge before I come to it. If cross-sections of the walls reach me, I can go ahead with the foundation . . . .

Mr. Kaufmann has told me the deadline is June 22nd, when he expects to have a big wedding anniversary.

Now the pace of construction continually threatened to embarrass the state of the plans. Hall wrote on January 24:

About finished on excavating today; will pour some footers today . . . .

Under separate cover I am showing you the size as I have scaled them. I can make some progress working at [the car-port] end of the building with favorable weather, while further plans are reaching me. I am making these plans that we may keep going. The set up is like this: I am down here on a salary. Mr. Kaufmann has gathered all his neighbors up, about twenty, that they may have some work this winter.

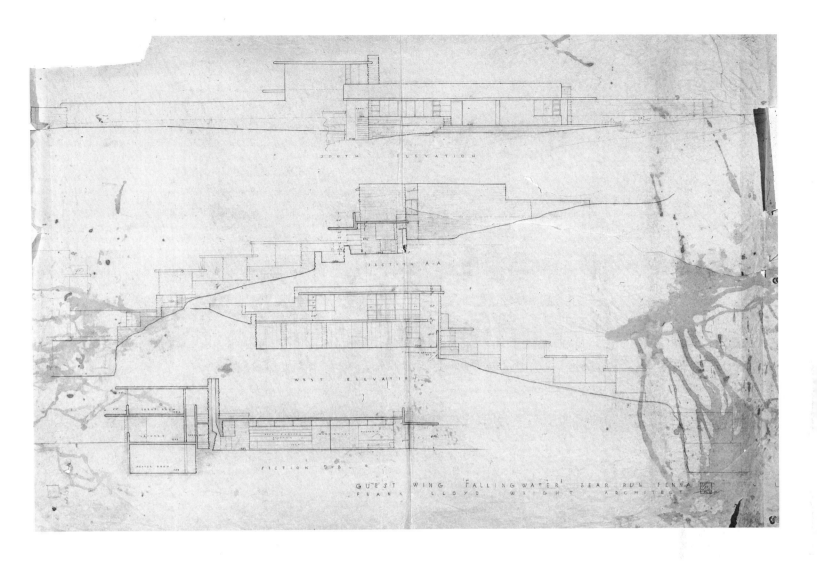

SOUTH ELEVATION

SECTION A-A

WEST ELEVATION

SECTION B-B

GUEST WING FALLINGWATER BEAR RUN PENNA
FRANK LLOYD WRIGHT ARCHITECT

Incidentally, they get twenty-five cents an hour. Mr. Kaufmann wants the house by June. I am trying to explain this situation to you that you might not answer me that I am supposed to build the building and not make the plans. Merely taking the position of Bob or Edgar if they were here.

Two days later, Wright sent Kaufmann some drawings "to help Hall along"; but the plans of January 26 were still preliminaries [98, 99]. Wright chose not to send an apprentice to serve as clerk-of-the-works. "We will cooperate to the best of our ability," he wrote Kaufmann, "but we are far away . . . If you get in a jam 'fly out.' "

Hall got caught in the middle, just as he feared. When he received a new contour map from Kaufmann's office, he discovered the servants' wing sited almost five feet past the line of his excavations. But he wrote Wright that he was glad to have the new drawings from Taliesin:

On Junior and Mr. Kaufmann's arrival on Sunday [January 29] we decided to put it [the new wing] back to the 91 feet . . . Mr. Kaufmann had the new drawings and I went over them thoroughly. To say the least I am happy to have this information, as I felt all the time I was going off half-cocked . . . .

I have about one-third of my stone out and have run into an eleven-inch course. This is a thicker stone than I had in the present house (Fallingwater). May I use the same for some of the coping and dot some of them in throughout the lower part of the wall? I have done this in my other work and like the effect.

He wrote Wright on February 4 that he would begin the stonework where there was the least mud, at the west end of the addition. "Ever since you built the Martin house," Hall said, "I have been keeping my buildings on the ground." Kaufmann thought the carports should be equipped with accordion wood doors; Wright sent a drawing on February 10, but wrote: "I recommend omitting these doors entirely as the shut-in car is a hangover from the folklore of capitalism." The next day, he begged Kaufmann to send him a "loan" of $1000.

Hall's situation at Bear Run quickly deteriorated, and he telegraphed Wright on February 18 that he was quitting. "Can't be yes-man other than to your plans," he wired. "Leaving job. Too many bosses. E. J. OK, but led by Jr. and Thumm." Later that weekend, Hall changed his mind. He wrote Wright on February 20:

> Lost my temper Saturday [February 18], but after Saturday and Sunday of sunshine and a talk with Mr. Kaufmann I'm feeling better. Hope things will run a little smoother.
>
> Wish to take back the statement that I was leaving. I fell in love with the job again, and cannot leave it. I must see circled stairs completed, inasmuch as I know they will be beautiful.
>
> Would like a penciled sketch of lintel stone in fireplace. I can get stone out now most any size.

If he was tired of Thumm and Edgar Kaufmann, jr., they in turn were perturbed by the absence of any clerk-of-the-works. The younger Kaufmann telegraphed Wright on February 20:

> We are badly in need of Edgar or whomever you want to send to get some of the most important stonework and other details launched. Please send someone right away.

Because the new wing was to be wholly in character with the main house, Wright thought he could watch over it well enough by receiving progress reports and construction photographs. The younger Kaufmann thought otherwise. He telegraphed Wright again, two days later:

> If you want addition built to your plans please acknowledge my last wire. Meantime I expect to see us get a Wright house, not a Hall house.

Wright responded the same day that Harold Turner would soon be in Pennsylvania for other work and could stop by "to see if he can't help get you started." Turner had built the hexagram or "Honeycomb" house in Palo Alto, California.

The final foundation plan reached Hall more than three weeks after he started the footings, and other drawings continued to fall behind. Wright insisted on making slight revisions, and they were always a good sign that he was pushing an idea to greater clarity and strength. Thumm nevertheless found him impossible. Angered by so many changes, he wrote the elder Kaufmann on March 1:

> In view of the fact that each drawing so far received from Mr. Wright is a change over the previous drawing means only one thing in my mind and that would be to shut down the job completely and wait until we can have final drawings, which will give definite information . . . .

> Willingly I have spent considerable time trying to properly decipher the architectural intent and thereby furnish Hall with the necessary field interpretation and dimensions in order that the work may progress; I have also spent considerable time with Metzger-Richardson in order to induce them to design the structural members (they gave up twice); the heating layout, along with other mechanical work . . . .
>
> There is further work to be done on all these subjects and it is not a matter of a few hours but days, and I feel it is a waste of time to collect the several component parts together into a building and then discard same to meet revised sets of drawings.
>
> . . . it does seem unethical and depressing to try to proceed and continue spending your money without any return . . . and when June comes we will not be done.
>
> What is the answer?

Hall, at least, stayed loyal; he wrote Wright on March 10 to report—contrary to Thumm—how well things were going:

> I had a talk with Mr. Kaufmann, giving me your telephone conversation. I was quite pleased that I have your moral support . . . .
>
> I have had a wonderful ten-day period of work: I have 30 men; half of the steel in first-floor guest part. I have forms up for garage roof, about 2/3 of the stone work completed.
>
> I have the job well organized and it is running smoothly. Plenty of willing help, with low wages. General labor: farmers and neighbors. I have the stone work up with cheap farmer masons, and I am quite happy over it, if it will only please you.

Wright seemed too busy to have time for Bear Run. He shortly left his winter camp in Arizona, traveled to Florida and Wisconsin, and toward the end of April set sail for London, where he was to hold the Sir George Watson chair of the Sulgrave Manor Board. He gave four lectures there in May. "No architectural speaker in London," it was reported, "has ever in living memory gathered such audiences. The atmosphere was charged with a strange expectancy . . . ."[10] During all the weeks Wright was away from his studio, Mosher and Tafel answered the questions from Bear Run and Pittsburgh. Most of them came from the dutiful Thumm and from Edgar Kaufmann, jr.

Hall had much of the new wing built before the revised drawings were finished on April 28; he worked as best he could with detail drawings and verbal directions from Taliesin. Wright made very little effort to visit the site. "I am sorry that you could not stop on your way home," Hall wrote on June 14. With all the changes and delays, the new wing could not be finished in time for the anniversary; and by the middle of July, when Hall visited Taliesin, he found

---

[10]See the introduction to *An Organic Architecture* (London, 1939).

Wright more eager to talk about four other residential commissions. Wright wanted his bids on all the projects, even though three were in Wisconsin.

The work at Bear Run trailed into August. "I am having an awful time getting cleaned up here," Hall wrote on August 11. "You can take this up with the various owners and see how they feel about it." Wright responded with a telegram on August 15: "Necessary to come here at once for arrangements if we are to build. Why make Kaufmann pay more?" Hall answered on August 20:

> I still have about a dozen men, and ought to get through this week. The Gillen men left Saturday [August 19]. A few changes, and plumbing and electrical work going on.
>
> Mr. Kaufmann expects to be back the latter part of the week. I just couldn't see how I could leave until his return, and see that everything was satisfactory. Built the guest house with very cheap labor, which requires a lot of my attention . . . .
>
> I figured the four plans which you sent me, and they seem to run $1,000 over your limits as I remember. I figured much better workmanship and materials than the Jacobs house [in Madison].
>
> I was in Philadelphia last week . . . and saw [Harold] Turner and the Sun Top apartments. Frankly, I wouldn't be very happy being pinned down to a lesser standard of material and workmanship . . . .
>
> I have about six boys that [I] have tried to teach the trade who have agreed to follow me for a year. Just how I could move them out to Wisconsin without some definite assurance of their starting to work at once doesn't seem feasible . . . .

Wright was due to meet Turner in Philadelphia on August 21, and he visited Bear Run a day or two later. Kaufmann, although exhausted, was happy to see him. "I always feel that I am a better man after having spent hours with you," he wrote on August 24, "and regret that our paths cross so seldom." They discussed the main house more than the new wing, and Kaufmann wrote of their agreement that "you will arrange to visit with us at least twice a year for a day and night so that we can have the benefit of your judgment and advice to keep the interior arrangement in harmony with your architectural creation."

The first week of September found Wright at his abysmal worst. He took advantage of his generous client and revenge on his loyal builder; he begged more money from Kaufmann and dismissed Hall forever. When he wrote Kaufmann on September 2 he juggled all the fees and payments, claimed a balance due of $4209.40 and then made so bold as to ask for $5000 in two installments:

> I hope this letter won't make you mad or anything like that but . . . I've been driven by the failure of the Lansing [Michigan] group of professors to get money—(seven houses for which we can yet get only a 3% preliminary fee although all

the plans are made) to see what I can do to tide over the emergency created in the Fellowship by their failure. As one hope I've been going over the work we've done for you.

> I meant to be generous with our resources where your work went, and I have been—to the limit and beyond, and always will be—I am now designing chairs, etc., etc., and getting a decent lighting for the place. I think I have it—meantime I've dug up five schemes I've drawn before—all lost in execution.
>
> . . . I am asking not for justice but mercy. So far you have paid me all I've asked but I haven't asked enough. You have no idea how much of our resources went into your work. If I had more I would have gladly given it to get for you and to give you the top—I am giving it here right now. I think you believe that . . . .
>
> Truth is, no money can be made by us to show for our time and effort at that figure but we've all got much besides to show for our time and effort—and—forever.
>
> Will you give us the lift?

Kaufmann answered on September 14:

> I sent you a telegram today telling you a check was going forward, but for your information your figuring is all cock-eyed. Although we have made complete settlement on the original house, the office and the guest wing, I still feel that your request is reasonable. So, I am, therefore, enclosing a check for $2500.

Hall, in good faith, was trying to finish at Bear Run; but Wright kept badgering him to start the houses in Wisconsin. The mistake Hall made was to suggest that Wright was accepting shoddy construction in his so-called Usonian houses.[11] "Have already lost three weeks waiting for you to make good," Wright telegraphed. "Now what? Do you walk out or walk in?" Finally, he wrote Hall on September 2:

> Cornelia [Brierly] tells me you are intending to build her aunts' house [in Pittsburgh] and have no intention of backing up your bids to the people here in Madison, having left us waiting to hear from you for more than three weeks—the summer slipping away and my duty to these clients therefore betrayed by you—because I depended on you.
>
> If this is the size and shape of your sense of responsibility I want nothing to do with you in any circumstances and object to entering into any contract with you on the Notz house [in Pittsburgh] if I have anything to do with it—you are no man to trust in that connection particularly.
>
> I learn that the real reason for your failure to keep your obligation to back up bids you made here at my request is because you have meantime been working on a Philadelphia prospect with your son—helping yourself as liberally as possible to my own material.

[11]In a conversation of May 30, 1981, at his home in New Hope, Pa., the late George Nakashima said he gave up architecture for woodworking after seeing the "Honeycomb House" and being dismayed by the discrepancy between Wright's order of design and its structural realization.

100. Gravel court near carports and servants' wing.

Strikes me as a pretty way to show appreciation and thanks for that. Were you to pitch in and help and earn something of a right and title to use me—I might feel differently.

As it is, you are just another exploiter.

Despite the simplicity of the new wing, and the low wages Kaufmann paid his neighbors, the costs grew out of proportion to those of the main house. Tardy drawings and frequent revisions caused too much waste, and Gillen inflated his charges for the millwork to retaliate for what Wright had called "the scalping of the bid he gave on the [main] house." Although the plan was scaled back from that of the year before, the new wing was far from impoverished. The narrow drive behind the main house doubled back in climbing the hill and passed through massive stone terminals to enter a gravel court, or "drying yard," planned on the 30–60 triangle: the same figure Wright had used to orient the main house [100]. The four carports were defined by stone piers canted at a 30-degree angle, and were screened from the main house by a long court wall and the laundry room. Above, there were two single servants' rooms and one double. Although they were small and served by a single bathroom, all were finished as if rooms in the main house; and, at Kaufmann's suggestion, the roof over the carports was paved with flags to make a terrace for the double room.

101. Stairway to servants' quarters.

The guests were screened by the stone chimney mass and the recessed stairway to the servants' quarters [101]. Their suite consisted simply of a "lounge," or living room, and a bedroom. Between the two were a bathroom, lighted and ventilated by a monitor; a short gallery with wardrobes, and an entryway lightly screened with wood stiles. The lounge, 23 feet long, provided a relaxed and comfortable space with a long and deep seat along the south window-wall that could be made into two more beds [102]. The discovery of larger stones in the quarry resulted in a splendid fireplace, striated as a revelation of the native sedimentary beds [103]. The mantel stone, or what Hall had called the lintel, was six feet long. In plan, the fireplace stepped back much like that in Mrs. Kaufmann's room, and again the same motif appeared close by in profile, in the staircase to the servants' quarters.

The bedroom in the guest suite was of modest size, about 13 feet north–south by 15 feet eight inches east–west [104]. But it opened through double doors of glass to a sunny terrace and—at long last—a swimming pool [105]. The stone steps into the water were wonderfully cantilevered [106]. Although the drawings of January 1939 showed the pool as

102. Guest-suite lounge.

OPPOSITE, TOP: 103. Lounge fireplace.

ABOVE: 104. Guest-suite bedroom.

OPPOSITE, BOTTOM: 105. Pool and terrace.

106. Cantilevered stones.

108. Cantilevered arbor and wisteria.

107. Stone masonry of terrace wall.

53 feet long, it was built much smaller: further evidence, no doubt, of Wright's resistance. Mrs. Kaufmann liked the pool at any size; at first, in the heat of summer, she favored the guest suite over the main house. She appreciated its greater seclusion and the cross-ventilation from the continuous clerestory at the north wall. Where the wall continued east to frame the terrace, Hall achieved some of the most beautiful masonry at Bear Run [107]. The stones had the vital and fleeting quality of sticks floating by in the stream, a perfect expression of Wright's belief in Heraclitus: "We can only know that all things are in process of flowing in some continuous state of becoming," Wright said that year in London.[12]

The sides of the pool were shaped like the parapets of the main house, swift and rounded at the edges, and the stone terrace continued in front of the guest bedroom, beneath a roof slab cantilevered about seven feet past the wall and perforated to become another trellis [108]. William Wesley Peters made the structural calculations. The slab, seven inches thick, was only six feet four and a half inches above the terrace but was folded upward to make the ceiling indoors seven feet nine and a half inches: another change of dimensions controlled by the 17-inch vertical unit.[13] The fold accomplished many things all at once; it strengthened

the cantilever, expanded the indoor space, maintained structural continuity and shaped an upper wall-face in complete harmony with the parapets of the main house.

Wright could easily have hidden the addition to Fallingwater off in the woods. Such, however, was not the discipline of his design. Because the privacy of both residences already was protected by the change in elevation and their distance apart, he made the new wing a child of the main house—one held by the hand. He linked the buildings with a stroke as graceful as it was daring, a semicircular walkway protected by a cantilevered canopy [109]. The canopy swooped down from the servants' entrance to the rock outcrop by the drive, returned in a separate reflex arc and met the bridgeway [110]. Perceived as a pattern of arcs, the largest struck from a radius about 28 feet distant, the canopied walk culminated all the curved details of the house. Where it ended at the bridge, a circular moss garden half indoors and half out became a period to the entire design [111].[14]

Wright once planned a double-deck bridge that would

[12]Wright, *An Organic Architecture*, p. 45.

[13]The lowest ceiling in the main house occurs at certain points of the third-story gallery and is 6′3¾″, although it was meant to be 6′4½″.

[14]In a letter of Oct. 5, 1976, Edgar Kaufmann, jr., indicated that the circular garden was not Wright's idea, although he approved it. Another moss garden is at the east end of the second-story landing, but entirely outdoors. Other planters for flowers or cuttings of rhododendron can be found at the south corners of the living room, east end of the hatch, in the metal "newel" at the second-story landing, on the third-story terrace (to conceal vents from the guest bathroom), at the plunge pool, at diagonally opposite terminals of the bridge over the stream, at the wall between the bridge and loggia, and by the guest-suite swimming pool.

BELOW: 109. Covered walkway.

OPPOSITE: 110. Walkway return and paved roof of bridge.

RIGHT: 111. Moss garden at bridge entrance.

112. Boulder at moss garden, with stone goddess from northeast India.

have entered the house at both upper stories. When the bridge was built at the second story only, the roof was paved with flags to become the walkway to an optional door at the third floor, never executed. Inside the bridge, a passage about 17 feet long, five skylights the same size as the lights in the bridge across the stream, 15 inches square, were likewise equipped with incandescent bulbs to serve as night lights. Near the moss garden, a boulder was allowed to penetrate the structure [112].

The semicircular canopy tripped down the hill in a final allusion to the falls. Vigorously cantilevered in folded planes, it recapitulated the structure of the main house. Mosher wondered how it could be supported by steel posts only at the circumference. Wright raised his forearm, bent his hand to the horizontal and demonstrated how difficult it was to push the hand any lower; but Peters had to make the actual calculations. The canopy was eight feet across and only three and one-half inches thick, half as thick as the roof slabs of the house, which so beautifully expressed shelter and the freedom Wright felt implicit in the horizontal. It acted somewhat as a ring beam, composed of half-inch bars running circumferentially and three other sizes of bars: a veritable weaving of steel in tension. It was the kind of structure Wright liked to compare with a spider's web.

The five slender steel posts that supported the main canopy stepped down from almost seven feet tall to less than four feet, and the single post of the reflex canopy was like a dwarf column, less than two feet tall. The posts were made of welded angles in three-fourths-inch plate. Their steel flanges introduced a spirited ornamental motif, a jagged profile repeated every eight inches as if to diagram how the columns were transferring loads of the canopy into the stone retaining wall of the walkway [113]. The flanges could also suggest the feathering of Indian arrows, just as the light-shields on the trellis beams—shaped as irregular pentagons, five inches at the top and three inches on each of the other sides—could be seen as an abstraction of Indian arrowheads.[15]

The ornamental range at Bear Run was so understated, so rigorously integrated with the very fabric of the building, it could easily escape notice. True ornament, Wright said, should exist as "the inherent melody of structure," as the "manifest *abstract pattern of structure itself.*"[16] Much of the

ornament at Bear Run was precisely that: the cantilevered metal shelves, the cantilevered wine sphere, the screens of the ceiling lights framed as if with a system of beams and joists, the cantilevered trellis beams, the energetically articulated furniture and the arcs and curved surfaces that everywhere responded to the plasticity of reinforced concrete.

113. Steel posts under canopy.

---

[15]The steel posts were painted Cherokee red. In his early years as an architect, Wright was particularly fond of the sculptures of Hermon A. MacNeil (1866–1947), who made Indians his subject-matter after seeing them perform at the World's Columbian Exposition of 1893. Wright designed his own Indian sculptures for his 1924 Nakoma Country Club project, which he called an "Indianesque affair." The shape of the wigwam inspired his slightly earlier Tahoe Summer Colony designs, just as he called the principal space of the Herbert F. Johnson house north of Racine, Wis., the "wigwam." Erich Mendelsohn wrote in 1924 that he had found Wright dressed in "a fantastic garment with something Indian about it . . . Bark shoes, a long staff, gloves and a tomahawk"; see *Letters of an Architect,* p. 73.

[16]*Frank Lloyd Wright on Architecture,* p. 236, and *An Autobiography,* p. 347 (his italics).

Changes in the hardware and lighting of the main house continued into 1939, and plans were made for screened areas on the living-room terraces, an idea of Kaufmann's that happily was abandoned. Kaufmann took great enjoyment in the house. "Things are humming here," he wrote Wright from his office, on October 18. "I cannot tell you how marvelous it is to be able to go to the country every week-end for a change." At the end of the month he sent the second check for $2500, and Wright responded: "I can't tell you how I appreciate your help where I guess I'll always need it most."

As they settled into their weekend house, the Kaufmanns gradually introduced various works of art, indoors and out. Wright gave them a few Japanese prints, but their tastes were more catholic than his, and the house proved fully accommodating. On later visits, Wright never made a sarcastic remark about the modernist sculptures, Edgar Kaufmann, jr., once wrote, although he "would invariably ask to have new statues relocated, often only a few feet from where they were . . . directing the sculpture into a telling position where it accentuated a feature of the architecture, and in turn gained the support of its setting."[17]

Engineers' reports on the deflections of the cantilevers continued at regular intervals: the third report, submitted in May 1940, noted "a further settlement of one quarter of an inch" but found the structure to be in "very good condition." Some of the hanger bars in the steps to the stream were described as bent, but it was assumed that the stress came only from heavy snow loads.

V. M. Bearer, the district forester who had inspected Bear Run in 1932, returned in 1940. In a report dated September 17, he suggested that black-walnut seedlings be planted in the occasional openings of the forest where charcoal hearths once had been operated. He was pleased by what he saw at Bear Run, and his pleasure must have been Kaufmann's too. "It is, indeed, gratifying to learn that my recommendations made eight years ago have been followed," Bearer wrote. "The area is well stocked with mixed hardwoods, laurel, rhododendron, hemlock and many shrubs. The clear, cold water of the swift and rocky Bear Run . . . helps makes this one of the finest areas in Pennsylvania."

Toward the end of World War II, while Edgar Kaufmann, jr., was serving with the Army Air Force, his parents engaged the Los Angeles architect Richard Neutra to design a winter house in Palm Springs, California. The younger Kaufmann was outraged when he first saw the blueprints and found that Wright was not the architect. Some years later, after the elder Kaufmann had become ill and by his son's account "captious," Wright designed another winter house for the family, for a site adjacent to that of the Neutra house. Wright said *his* house could bring the

family back together. Desert boulders were scattered all about the well-clipped lawn of the Neutra house, but Wright conceived a house with boulders in the walls—a gentle echo, perhaps, of the larger and more rugged boulders at Bear Run. On January 15, 1951, he wrote Liliane Kaufmann:

> The house for the queen is designed. Boulder House it is . . . Feminine in essence; broad as the hills in feeling. I will get you out of the nasty nice cliché [the Neutra house] with a fine sweep.
>
> I hope you all rise to that outdoor-indoor sweep . . . .

He wrote her again on February 9. "It is no ordinary opus I have worked out," he said, "but a prescription for genuine Kaufmann unity and happiness—real relief." Mrs. Kaufmann was not so optimistic about the healing powers of architecture—even Wright's—but she thanked him for his sentiments. Planned with segments of circles and their reflexes, the house of boulders would have placed Wright's architecture in direct competition with the International Style, or what Neutra chose to call his "biorealism."[18] Wright remained especially fond of his design. "It was a rare and beautiful thing," he wrote E. J. Kaufmann in July 1953. "One of my very best."

It was also toward the end of the war that Kaufmann thought again about adding a servants' sitting-room to the kitchen of the house on Bear Run. The kitchen measured only 15 feet six inches by 12 feet two inches, and was the only space in the house without distinctive quality. Kaufmann had asked Wright about adding to the kitchen as early as November 1935; by now, he did not intend to ask. Edgar Kaufmann, jr., interceded about a year later, and virtually took charge. "The alterations for Bear Run are all drawn up," he wrote Wright on July 22, 1946. He reported again on September 4:

> I have just come back from three days at Bear Run. I believe you would be really content with the present shape of the alterations undertaken after my talk with you. Both of them look completely easy and natural in with the old house, and the little sitting room in particular has an unusually agreeable air. It seems to arrange a flow of space in and around the new cellar stairs in an admirable way, and these

[17]Edgar Kaufmann, jr., "The Fine Arts and Frank Lloyd Wright," in *Four Great Makers of Modern Architecture* (New York, 1963), p. 35.

[18]For the Boulder House, see *Frank Lloyd Wright in His Renderings 1887– 1959,* ed. Yukio Futagawa (Tokyo, 1984), figs. 162, 163, and *Frank Lloyd Wright Monograph 1951–1959,* ed. Yukio Futagawa (Tokyo, 1988), figs. 38–40. Richard Neutra (1892–1970), a Viennese, came to America in 1923, met Wright in April 1924 at the funeral of Louis H. Sullivan, and soon spent several months at Taliesin. For his Kaufmann house in Palm Springs—which at last provided the client with a large swimming pool— see Arthur Drexler and Thomas S. Hines, *The Architecture of Richard Neutra* (New York, 1982), pp. 100–103, or Esther McCoy, *Richard Neutra* (New York, 1960), figs. 51–55. "This is a house that is partaking of the dynamic changes around it," Neutra said of the Kaufmann house in a lecture at the University of Kansas on March 13, 1963. "This building is changing. It is oriented into the landscape. It is underlining, with its simple geometric forms, the ruggedness of the mountain-scape."

stairs themselves are noticeably lighter than before. Since we keep the extra ice-box down below, it is especially pleasant to have this a good part of the house for those who use it . . . .

Although the sitting room, only about ten feet square, became an inconspicuous addition, it clearly lacked Wright's special touch and the benefit of his unerring eye for proportions. The large mitred-glass window at the salient south corner [114] was without any articulation, the casement at the east corner was oversized and the narrow window that presented an unexpected view of the boulder beneath the west bedroom terrace abutted a grotesquely miniature stone wall.

Usually, the Kaufmanns entertained only a few guests at Bear Run; but with larger groups they found the entryway and the dining area too cramped. They mentioned this to Wright late in 1946. About a year later he began plans for extending the house into the drive and for adding a "Shady Lane" entrance with another row of carports higher on the hill, above the servants' wing.

The plans came to nothing. In fact they represented the first in a long series of commissions destined not to be built. Wright was well paid, and once Kaufmann sent him a new car, unannounced, as a Christmas gift; but he grew much discouraged. He was in his eighties, and it was getting too late, he said, to be expending his best efforts on projects never realized. Kaufmann had him at work in 1947 and 1948 on vast and variant designs for the development of Point Park, in Pittsburgh, into a constellation of bridges, highways, towers and such civic amenities as theaters, an aquarium and—reminiscent of their earliest discussions in 1934–a planetarium. In 1949 and 1950 Wright designed two versions of a self-service parking garage connected to the department store, which had merged with the May Company of New York in October 1946. It, too, would have been an impressive structure in coiling ramps of reinforced concrete. After the Boulder House came a "Rhododendron Chapel" at Bear Run, a project Wright conceived early in 1952 as a place for meditation and agent of family harmony. It looked overscaled, as though meant for services;

114. Servants' sitting-room, added to main house.

the faceted glass walls recalled his project of 1926 for a great steel cathedral "for a million people," in New York. In 1952 and 1953 Wright designed for Kaufmann two versions of a "Point View" apartment tower in Pittsburgh, and for Edgar Kaufmann, jr., in 1956 and 1957 he worked on plans for a gate lodge, service court and television antenna-tower at Bear Run.[19]

Except during the war years, when the house was closed to conserve fuel and the Kaufmanns used a small roadside house instead, the engineers continued to measure the deflections. In May 1950 they reported that the roof of the covered terrace had moved about an inch and a half lower than the year before. Roy M. Oliver, who had succeeded Thumm as superintendent of the store buildings and was likewise obliged to attend to Bear Run, sent the report to Wright. In September, after an earlier attempt to jack the roof merely depressed the floor, a post was inserted between the roof and the parapet. Five slender bars were added later, and a second post was installed in July 1953, much more obtrusively; another post, beneath it, rested on the stair wall by the plunge pool. After further "signs of distress" were observed, the east part of the roof was rebuilt in September 1954.

Kaufmann still heard from the engineers in the last weeks of his life. In a report of March 9, 1955, they said the window glass by the stairs to the stream had shattered, the mullions were no longer plumb and the doors to the east living-room terrace refused to open readily. All were deemed signs of progressive settlement. The conclusion was politely ominous:

> we believe that for some years this structure has been quietly asking for help (by bending stair hangers, twisting frames and breaking glass) and that in the near future it will demand assistance in a more forceful manner.

Kaufmann relished his long association with Wright, despite all the conflicts and worries, and he knew very well the value of what they had brought into being. He had long suffered ill health. On April 15, 1955, a few hours after a visit from Wright, he died at the Palm Springs house.[20] Liliane Kaufmann, who had died at Bear Run on September 7, 1952, once sent Wright a birthday greeting in which she wrote: "Living in a house built by you has been my one education—and for that and for the privilege of knowing you, I will always be grateful." For his part, Wright had saluted Kaufmann in a letter of February 25, 1950. "I conceived a love for you quite beyond the ordinary relationship of client and Architect," he wrote. "That love gave you Fallingwater."

Now it was up to Edgar Kaufmann, jr., to keep the house from being compromised by the reinforcements so regularly proposed by the Pittsburgh engineers. A flood in the fall of 1954 had damaged the stairs to the stream, and in the summer of 1955 he had plans made to carefully strengthen the steps. Two steel angle bars were carried down into the bedrock close to the original ties (T-bars, welded back to back), and the two hangers of the bottom tread were eliminated. The change was slight, and indeed it improved the design. A much more severe storm and flood assaulted the house in August 1956, as Edgar Kaufmann, jr., has recounted:

> Water rose far above the living room floor, and although the terrace doors kept most of it out, the bridge to the guest wing was more leaky. The stairs became a cascade. The wind was violent and of course all wires were down. Worse, the house was hung with pendant scaffoldings of heavy timber, as we had begun to repaint. The scaffolding was caught in the wind and shook the whole house like a terrier shakes a rat. I was there (it was a week-end) and felt sure that somewhere something must snap. To release the scaffolding was impossible, its nails were tightly gripped by the water-soaked timbers. There was nothing to do but pile up the furniture and wait. In four or five hours the storm abated. The damage to the property was enormous; to the house, nil; only much cleaning of mud and sand was required.[21]

Frank Lloyd Wright was nearly 92 years old when he died on April 9, 1959, in Phoenix. For several more years, Edgar Kaufmann, jr., continued to use the house on Bear Run; but in September 1963 he announced his intention of giving it to the public, under the care of the Western Pennsylvania Conservancy, of Pittsburgh. The house and 1543 acres surrounding it were formally accepted in a ceremony on October 29 as "The Kaufmann Conservation on Bear Run, a Memorial to Edgar J. and Liliane S. Kaufmann."[22] That day, Edgar Kaufmann, jr., looked back on his years with the house:

> Its beauty remains fresh like that of the nature into which it fits. It has served well as a home, yet has always been more than that: a work of art, beyond any ordinary measures of excellence . . . House and site together form the very image of man's desire to be at one with nature, equal and wedded to

[19]For the new entrance scheme and the Rhododendron Chapel, see *Frank Lloyd Wright: Drawings for a Living Architecture* (New York, 1959), pp. 91, 92. The Point Park projects, *Frank Lloyd Wright Preliminary Studies 1933–1959*, ed. Yukio Futagawa (Tokyo, 1987), figs. 238–251, *Frank Lloyd Wright Monograph 1942–1950*, ed. Yukio Futagawa (Tokyo, 1988), figs. 376–388, and *Frank Lloyd Wright in His Renderings*, figs. 148, 149 and 152. The parking-garage projects, *Frank Lloyd Wright Monograph 1942–1950*, figs. 538–544, and *Frank Lloyd Wright in His Renderings*, fig. 158. The Point View apartment projects, *Frank Lloyd Wright Monograph 1951–1959*, figs. 115–123 and 196–200, and *Frank Lloyd Wright in His Renderings*, fig. 170. And for the gate lodge project, *Frank Lloyd Wright Monograph 1951–1959*, figs. 494–498.

[20]See the *Pittsburgh Post-Gazette*, April 16, 1955, pp. 1, 4, and 5.

[21]"Twenty-five Years of the House on the Waterfall," *L'architettura—cronache e storia*, 82 (Aug. 1962), p. 42.

[22]Since then, the Conservancy has increased the site to 4600 acres, to safeguard the Bear Run watershed. Founded in 1931 as a private nonprofit organization, the Conservancy primarily seeks to acquire land suitable for state parks and nature reserves.

nature . . . Such a place cannot be possessed. It is a work by man for man, not by a man for a man . . . By its very intensity it is a public resource, not a private indulgence.[23]

Having introduced the house in January 1938 with a photographic exhibition, The Museum of Modern Art now celebrated its new public status by commissioning Ezra Stoller to photograph it afresh, in color. The pictures were exhibited at the museum from November 3 to December 1.

[23]Edgar Kaufmann, jr., died in July 1989 at 79.

Many years later, the *Architectural Record* conducted a poll to choose for its centennial issue of July 1991 the most important buildings of the last hundred years. Fallingwater took first place.

As a work of art, the house on Bear Run reveals itself slowly, unpredictably and never once and for all. It is a wonderful building even in bad weather, and it is wonderful at night [115, 116]. There was never any house quite like it before, and there has been none since.

115. Fallingwater in rain.

116. Fallingwater at dusk, late 1937.

Index

Page numbers in *italics* refer to illustrations only.